A SURVIVOR'S CLOSET

How my memories as a little girl became the diary of one of the most horrific, severe child abuse stories in Missouri history.

Debra M. Luptak
Edited by Victoria Giraud, CA.

A SURVIVOR'S CLOSET:
How my memories as a little girl became the diary of one of the most horrific, severe child abuse stories in Missouri history.

ISBN: 0-9728711-1-X (Paperback)
ISBN: 0-9728711-0-1 (Hardcover)

Library of Congress Control Number: 2003090779

First Printing: February 2003

Printed in the United States of America
Minneapolis, Minnesota

This book is printed on acid free paper.

A note from the author:

I know there are more gifted writers in the world than myself; however, it is my hope that you can overlook the imperfections that may be contained within.

This is my true story spoken from the heart, and I believe no one else could tell it. When you have gone through a childhood such as mine, the least of your worries is a misplaced comma or a run-on sentence.

My most important objectives in writing this story were to break the silence, create awareness of child abuse severity in our society, and support the millions of other victims who still remain in silence.

TABLE OF CONTENTS

v

ACKNOWLEDGEMENTS

Throughout my life I have encountered many wonderful people who supported and guided me along the roughest roads of my life. My deepest appreciation goes to a professional and caring therapist, Gael Entrikin of Lutheran Social Services of Minnesota, who helped me for over twenty-six years.

I will always be indebted to my loving and supportive children, Brian and Melissa Haugen, Shannon and Devon Haugen, and Bryce and Shawn Haugen. I also want to express my gratitude to my former husband of twenty years, Kent, for his patience and compassion along the way. I thank the many friends I've made, as they held me up when I had no strength to walk alone. Thank you for encouraging me when you knew I was strong enough to take flight, your support will always remain in my heart.

Thank you to my very loving and patient husband Stephen, my angel, a very blessed man who every day nurtures only "light" into our world. And thanks to my very dear friends, Steve and Pat, who continually influence and encourage me to reach for my dreams. My gratitude goes out to a wonderful woman, Raven, for her loyal friendship, her many spiritual gifts, her blessings and prayers she continues to send. Thank you to Sage, who married and blessed us, who has been my sounding board through tough times, bringing to my awareness what I wasn't always able to realize on my own. The inspiration, encouragement and prayers from all of you have helped me to continue to believe in myself and love myself.

I would also like to acknowledge my Editor, Victoria Giraud, and my marketing company, Media Relations, Inc., for their constructive guidance in the writing and publishing process. The emotional connection during editing, the personal attention to my interests and your patience went far beyond the call of duty.

Many people throughout my life have contributed to making my experience of writing this book an enjoyable and exciting endeavor and for that I say, "Thank

You…I could not have done this without your encouragement!"

For those of you who take offense to my story, I have one simple comment to add…"Each of us is blessed with very different eyes and hearts; therefore, no two individuals were intended to see or feel the world the same." This book is written through my child's eyes and heart, my world.

My last acknowledgement goes to my "Angels," who have taught me to Love myself. They have followed me and given me protection and guidance toward finding my inner peace and spiritual energies.

PREFACE

This book is written for the many people in the world who are searching to center their spirits and find inner peace. I hope each of you will take away a special gift, seen or unforeseen, by reading my book. Join me in my journey as I show you what it took for me to truly heal and learn to love myself. I hope I have helped you in your own search to prevail. Courage and hope endures all.

Throughout the book, I will share and describe graphic details of the tortures, beatings and near death experiences that happened during my childhood. During my life I have walked many dark paths and acquired my own wisdom. I found I had a special gift for survival and will share these experiences with you. My story has a special ending, as I relate how I became a courageous adult and turned my childhood hell into a gift to help others.

May this book help you identify with some important issues in your own life or with someone close to you. I hope you will truly hear my words in the later chapters and allow them to absorb into pieces of your own life.

It is my intent throughout this book to provide you with child abuse insights for tackling your own issues or others around you who may be the victim or the perpetrator of child abuse. Learning and realizing how to take on those tougher challenges of childhood makes us stronger beings. You cannot change what you do not acknowledge. All too often we get caught up in our painful past because it's all we know, not realizing there is a better life for us. I hope my book will help you realize there is a better life for you.

I envision you, my reader, sitting quietly in a café or coffee shop on an early, dewy morning as the sun is just beginning to rise, or maybe during a warm sunny afternoon, savoring a large Latte, Cappuccino or Mocha, while reading my book, enjoying my personal story I have chosen to share with you. When you relate to a certain chapter, paragraph or sentence, may it bring a smile to your face or chills to your skin because of realism. Soon you will realize that you too can be a conqueror, not just a survivor in your own life.

INTRODUCTION:

Just Another Day

It was just another scorching hot summer day in Arizona and the routine of the day was about to begin. My sister Danielle and I were confined to a van, where my mother and new stepfather, Harold, a retired Army Lieutenant Colonel, forced us to live and sleep, keeping us hidden away when we were not being forced to pick up stones and brush from their desert property.

The van doors were jerked open with a loud whack. Outside on the sandy ground stood my mother and

Harold with their usual fuming looks, something my sister Danielle and I had learned to live with. Harold jumped up into the van and grabbed both of us by the hair, dragged us to the edge of the van door and then pushed us out onto the rough desert ground simultaneously. As Harold jumped out of the van, he and my mother picked us off the ground by our hair. With Harold gripping my hair and my mother gripping Danielle's hair, they dragged us across the sandy yard to the spot where my two brothers, my sister Danielle and I always began our mornings.

Fear struck me, as I repeatedly asked myself each day, "What is going to happen next? What are they going to do to us today?" We were prisoners of Harold and my mother.

At the time I was seven years old and Danielle was six, Matthew was eight and Mark was four. My two-year-old sister, Doreen, was not a part of our punishing routines as she was just a toddler.

As I stood in line, I couldn't control my trembling as I watched Harold pace back and forth in front of us. He stopped and stood in front of me, glaring with evil eyes. His large hand grabbed me by my hair and lifted me off the ground. In a very powerful motion Harold twisted me around in a circular motion, as if I were a rag doll, and kicked the breath out of me. He dropped me to the ground when he was finished teaching me that he was the boss and I was going to learn to respect him.

This was just another day in Harold's prison, a ten-acre site that was surrounded by a barrier wall of dual tractor tires to keep others out. After my beating, Harold shouted for all of us to get to work. I ran for my bucket so I could begin walking the grounds to pick up stones and brush. I knew if I didn't dash to get to work, another beating would occur.

Matthew and Mark were ordered to water and feed the horses and dogs. Since my sister and I were considered less than animals, if we were to eat, we had to sneak food from the animals to feed ourselves. When Harold wasn't watching I would secretly grab handfuls of dog food from the piles that lay on the ground.

For a year Harold had begun our day with his routine torture. More always followed, but half the fear was not the beatings themselves, but never knowing what was next. One of his disciplinary measures included large sheets of tin placed on the ground to absorb the sun's merciless heat. By noon the Arizona sun had scorched the tin to 100 degrees and hotter. Yelling at the top of his lungs, Harold ordered us girls over to the sheets of tin that had been baking in the sun all morning. Harold wanted to teach us not to run away, and as part of our punishment he also took away our little tennis shoes. We were forced to walk around the desert ground barefoot without protection from the earthly elements. Harold once again grabbed us by the back of the hair and placed each of us in front of one of the sheets of hot tin. He would force us to slowly walk across the scorching sheets; he never hesitated to point a gun at our heads if we protested. As we slowly walked across the tin, we had to try and hide the fiery pain, but I couldn't help but scream as I took each new step to get to the other side of the tin sheet. It felt like miles before I reached the other side, only to see Mother's face and large body standing at the other end, with the cattle prod in her hand, ready to use it if I didn't turn around and repeat the walk once again.

After completing this horror, Harold ordered my sister and I back into the hot, stuffy van where we were to remain and not come out unless called. Although it was hot and stuffy, we dashed for the van where we knew we would not have to feel any pain. The torture was over for now.

On this particular day, Harold shouted a summons for all of us in mid afternoon. Danielle and I immediately opened the back doors of the van and jumped out. Harold shouted orders for all of us children to get into the station wagon because we were going to town.

I was totally confused with this new development as I ran for the station wagon and jumped in the back with Danielle. Since our mother dressed us in identical clothing, I believed we were twins. We always stood side-by-side and clung to each other as we were waiting for the next command. Somehow our clinging bodies became our emotional support and courage to obey their orders.

Harold drove the station wagon while Mother was in the passenger seat holding my baby sister, Doreen.

The rest of us kids rode in the back. Where we were going and what was going to happen, I wondered as I stared out the window? In a short time we arrived at a large parking lot, vehicles were everywhere, quite a contrast to our lonely desert prison. Harold opened the back hatch of the vehicle and sternly ordered us to jump out. The four of us followed Harold and Mother, who was carrying Doreen, as they headed into a large building.

Silently we were led into a small room. The floor was covered with colorful objects of all shapes and sizes, things that were unfamiliar to all of us. The five of us got down on the floor to immediately explore and discover all the toys. Since we had never had toys, we stared at them in amazement, wondering what to do with them. Since Harold and Mother were not in the room, I forgot my worries and just enjoyed the toys.

Not long afterwards, the door of the playroom opened. My mother, Harold, and a lady who was a stranger entered the room. I wondered who she was and why she was there as I stopped playing to stare at her. I remember the emotions that ran through my body when I saw her. I had a strong feeling that I wanted to secretly tell her that my parents were being mean to my sister and me. I wanted to whisper to her to help us. I wanted to tell her that our parents beat and tortured us and that we cried and had pain every day. I wanted to tell her I was so hungry and all I got to eat was dog food I sneaked from the animals. I know the look on my face was silently begging this woman without a single word coming from my mouth. I knew I couldn't say a word in front of my mother and Harold or there would be another beating when we returned home.

As the lady walked into the room, she observed each of us children playing on the floor together. "Debra and Danielle, will you come with me?" she asked us kindly.

I looked up at her in amazement that she knew our names. I was confused; what did she want from us? Looking over at my mother and Harold for direction, my mother ordered with her screeching voice, "Debra and Danielle go with the lady."

I jumped up. I knew if I didn't obey her, my mother and Harold would punish me later. Danielle and I followed the lady to the door of the playroom. Just before the door closed, I turned back and looked at my brothers and my baby sister, Doreen, who remained playing on the floor. I knew somewhere deep within my soul that I would probably never see them again. I was flooded with emotions of sadness. I felt unloved, singled out and abandoned. The questions were spinning in my head so fast. It was like something was dying inside of me, as I was being forced once again to do something that didn't feel right. The door closed behind me.

Holding hands, Danielle and I followed the nice lady down a long hallway past desks and secretaries that lined both sides. As we followed, I turned to look back at the room where my brothers and baby sister were. I wanted to go back. A rush of pain and sadness came over me as I began to scream and cry, "Let me go back to my family." Danielle began to cry with me. It was then that I knew I would never see my family again. My heart sunk as I cried again to the lady, "Please let me go back to my family."

This painful day, which started out as just another day, became a day of desertion. The pain, the tears,

the sadness and loss were more then I had ever imagined my body could endure. Even the beatings and
torture never caused pain to my heart the way this
day did.

Danielle and I had been dumped off at a Social Services Office in Maricopa County, Arizona. We were
to be placed in a foster home together. We never saw
our family again.

CHAPTER ONE

Conception

My father, Larry, was from a prominent Catholic family residing in the suburbs of St. Louis, Missouri. He was a handsome young man, who stood 5'6" tall and weighed as little as 160 pounds. With a small frame and dark brown hair, Larry was attractive to women, but he had little interest in them. When he graduated from high school at eighteen, his passion was to enlist in the Marines, where he became an engine repairman.

His parents, Larry senior and Gretchen, were educated, prominent and well-known artists in Missouri. As responsible parents, they always encouraged their three children, Larry, Jennifer and Loretta, to pursue their educations.

Larry senior began painting at the age of eleven and painted throughout his life. His work included land-scapes, still life and portraits in watercolor, oil and acrylic, as well as woodcarvings, and his work has been displayed throughout the United States. In style and composition, Larry senior, who worked with brush and palette knife, was truly an original. He was a member of the St. Louis County Art Association. Exhibits, receptions and private showings of his paintings were held at the Government Center, St. John's Mercy Hospital and the Missouri Botanical Garden.

They lived just outside of the city on a small hobby farm, where my father, Larry junior, had a favorite pony. He and his sisters, Jennifer and Loretta, enjoyed the freedom of country living.

Larry junior chased his dreams by joining the Marines and traveling all over the world by sea for four years. When Larry came home to St. Louis for the

Christmas holidays in 1958, he was introduced to an attractive young woman named Jayne while attending a local dance. Jayne's mother insisted that Larry and her daughter get acquainted. There was something unique about Jayne that sparked Larry's attention. She was a pretty woman who stood 5'9" tall, and she had short, jet-black hair and stunning hazel blue eyes. Home on leave, and dating a new woman, he soon realized he had to make a decision whether to continue in the Marines or stay at home, look for work and settle down. The young couple, finding they had common interests, began a serious relationship. They were delighted when they discovered their families lived close to each other in nearby suburbs.

Jayne came from a very demanding family. Her mother, a very large aggressive woman, was afflicted with a bipolar disorder, also known as a manic-depressive. Jayne and her sister, Pam, were forced to cater to their mother's profound illness while her brother was free to grow up without that responsibility. Jayne's mother wanted her daughter's undivided attention at all times and would order Jayne to wait on her, bringing her drinks or cigarettes or whatever else she demanded. After years of emotional and verbal abuse by her mother, Jayne was looking forward to leaving her mother's side and starting a new life of her own.

Wedding bells rang November 1959 in the Catholic Church as Larry and Jayne were united. Young at heart, they anticipated a lifetime of joy ahead of them. Larry worked in the downtown courthouse as a Clerk of Courts and Jayne stayed at home as a housewife. It wasn't long before there was an announcement to their families that they were expecting their first child. When they privately discussed choosing the name of their first newborn, Jayne refused to consider picking out a girl's name. Young and inexperienced, Larry thought nothing of his wife's stubborn refusal.

Matthew was born on a warm, sunny day in September 1960, and Larry and Jayne felt blessed with happiness.

When Matthew was only a few months old, one day Jayne laid him on the kitchen countertop, instructing him to stay on the counter and not to move. A normal, active baby, Matthew rolled off the counter and onto the floor. When Jayne picked Matthew up from the floor, she scolded him for falling off the counter. She told Larry about the incident when he returned home from work that evening, but he was not alarmed, innocently thinking to himself that accidents do happen and Jayne was of course a new mother.

CHAPTER TWO

Unwanted Child

Eleven months later a second birth was about to arrive. Faced with the decision of a name for their second child, my mother once again refused to consider a girl's name. My father wondered why his wife refused to talk about the fifty-fifty chance of having a girl, but he dropped the issue, keeping his thoughts to himself. On a September day in 1961, my father and mother brought a second child into the world, a daughter this time. When my mother continued to refuse to name their new daughter, my father decided to name me Debra Marie.

When they brought me home from the hospital, my mother wasn't shy about her feelings of extreme displeasure with me, as she ignored my cries for care. Bewildered, my father began to wonder why his wife was unhappy with their new daughter.

Mother was a full time mother, now caring for two children in a small home next door to my father's parents' home, Larry senior and Gretchen. Antagonistic toward me, Mother decided that a small closet in the back of the house would serve as my room, and put my crib in the closet.

My mother refused to hold or nurture her new baby girl. When I would cry from hunger or from a wet diaper, my mother ignored my cries and avoided taking care of my infant needs. I would remain in the same diaper, sometimes for a week at a time until deep sores developed on my bottom. When my mother could no longer ignore my cries, she would force her hand or a blanket over my face and yell at me to stop crying.

Our family home was located in a swampy, wooded area. At three weeks old a mosquito had bitten me.

The bite caused me to run a high fever, which caused convulsions, and then I slipped into a coma. My father rushed me to the hospital and I was diagnosed with encephalitis, which meant I had to have my spine drained, followed by weeks of recovering in the hospital.

During this stay in the hospital, my mother kept insisting to my father that I was born crazy and that ever since she brought me home as a newborn, she had known there was something wrong with me.

On a hot summer day after I had recovered and returned home from the hospital stay another tragic incident occurred. Father was mowing the lawn in the front yard of our home when suddenly my mother hysterically ran out of the house with me, a six-week-old baby, draped over her arms, yelling, "Debra is dying, Debra is dying."

Shocked by the ruckus, my father instantly stopped the mower engine, ran up to my mother and grabbed me from her arms. He dashed for the house where he laid me on the living room floor, giving me mouth-to-mouth resuscitation. By this time I had stopped breathing and was turning blue from lack of oxygen to my brain. My father yelled at my mother "Call an ambulance!" but instead my mother ran over to my father's parents' home next door to tell them that I was dead. My grandparents called an ambulance in their attempt to save my life.

The ambulance arrived to find a six-week-old baby girl blue, unconscious and not breathing. While working diligently to revive me, the ambulance rushed me to the hospital for further medical treatment.

During the ride to the hospital, the ambulance staff prepared the paperwork for the emergency call. As part of the accident report, the ambulance doctors asked my father and mother, who were also riding in the ambulance, what had happened? My mother replied to the ambulance staff, "Debra tried to kill herself."

"Now, Miss, what really happened?" asked one of the incredulous ambulance drivers.

My father looked at his wife, thinking the story was impossible, but my mother continued to insist that I had stuck my blanket down my throat, trying to commit suicide. Father yelled at my mother, begging her to tell the truth. Mother repeatedly insisted her story was exactly what had happened and that is what they were to write down on the report.

While I was in the hospital recovering from Mother's version of a suicide attempt, my father was able to visit me at the end of each day when he left work. During one of Father's visits, while putting his name and the time down on the parents' sign-in sheet, he noticed that my mother had not once visited me. But when he approached my mother and asked her if she had gone to visit Debra that day, she told him, "I go and see Debra every day." Although my father was very upset over what was happening to his family and my mother's erratic ongoing behavior, he avoided any further confrontation with my mother.

As I grew older, my mother believed I was "queer" because I was always fondling myself. In reality, I was rubbing at open sores, the result of soggy diapers that seldom got changed. To solve what my mother believed to be the real problem, she had sewn a type of straitjacket to restrain my arms and legs. This confining, handmade restraint kept my left leg crossed over my right leg and kept my arms crossed as well. It did the trick and kept my hands out of my diapers. When my father confronted my mother to remove me from this device, she told him, "Debra was playing with herself and the straitjacket stops her." Walking away in disgust, shaking his head in disbelief, my father once again avoided confrontation and let my mother have her way.

After several months of being in Mother's home-sewn straitjacket, I was unable to stand in my crib as a normal child would have, as they begin to pull themselves up using the side rails of a crib. I managed to roll over but couldn't find the strength to pull myself up. Although my father was aware of my difficulties, he wasn't sure how to stop Mother's persistently strange and bizarre tactics of motherhood.

When my father came home from work at night, my mother would greet my father at the doorway and immediately force Matthew, my older brother, into his arms. My father would then question her, "Where is Debra?"

My mother would become extremely upset and begin yelling at my father. "Why are you so interested in your daughter? I told you at the hospital when Debra was born that she is part of the devil and that is why she cries all the time. She is in her closet, you don't need to go in there; leave her alone."

My mother's glaring, large round face framed by dark black hair remains instilled in my memory. Her face, along with her voice, lived as darkness within my body. The feelings that overcame me when I saw her face as a young child, the fear and terror each time I looked up at her has continued to live in my emotional tissue and probably will forever.

My mother repeatedly yelled at me, "You are evil, you are a part of the devil." She would shout throughout the house, "Your father is a part of the devil and so are you." This message remains instilled in my memory.

My mother's delusional beliefs were powerful in her mind. She profoundly believed that I was a part of the devil, born out of evil. My father struggled with my mother's distorted thoughts and strange behavior toward me, while watching my mother's loving behavior toward my brother, Matthew, the opposite end of the spectrum. After months of ongoing trauma between his wife's behavior and the torture of his daughter, my father finally sought the counsel of family members and their local Catholic priest.

Their family priest responded, "Have faith, Jayne will be healed, and in the meantime keep the family together." Divorce was not an option for my father, according to his priest.

As my father spoke privately to different family members, they reminded him that his faith would prevail against the darkness his family was going through. Family members even undermined the credibility of my father's story because they refused to believe what was happening. With their denial and standoffish responses, my father was once again struggling to find someone to listen to him and help him take action to stop this nightmare happening to his family.

CHAPTER THREE

Mother's Torment

Eleven months after I was born, my sister Danielle came into the world on an August day in 1962. Yet again, Mother refused to name or accept her new, second daughter. Home videos of my brother, Matthew, were the joy of Mother's world, but something inside her continually blocked her motherly instincts to nurture and love her daughters, Danielle and myself.

My father always had a love for home improvement projects—painting, remodeling and just fixing up the house. This was my father's hobby. But my mother's need for attention and jealousy had always managed to get in the way of her ability to care for her daughters.

One day while painting the back porch, my father tried to ignore my mother's screaming and nagging at him. Finally he gave up and threw his bucket of paint up into the air, and the paint landed all over my mother. Splattered full of wet paint, my mother's anger took over. She immediately called her father and brother, who lived nearby, telling them they needed to come and protect her since my father was beating and slapping her. Despite my father's protests, the police, who had been summoned by my grandfather, believed my mother's claims of abuse and took control of the situation by handcuffing my father and taking him off to jail for the night.

On days when my father went off to work, my mother would take his carpentry hand tools and forcefully drive them into the ground in the backyard. When he came home in the evening, he would ask, "Why are my tools all driven into the ground in the backyard?"

My mother would lead him out to the yard and furiously point to the tools and insist in screaming tones, "Danielle and Debra did this today and are being punished for their bad behavior." My father knew that his two small daughters could not have had the force or strength to drive tools into the ground.

My mother was continually seeking attention, usually negative, by destroying something and blaming it on her tiny daughters. When my father laid new carpet, my mother decided to wear high heels in the living room on the new carpet. When he got home, he noticed snags all over the carpet and asked her how they got there. Once again she blamed Danielle and me. "The girls are nothing but trouble, you need to punish them," she told him.

If my mother and her sister Pam went shopping on a Saturday afternoon, my mother would make sure my father did the babysitting. She told him that Danielle and I were down for a nap for the day and that he was not for any reason to go into our room; he could only play and entertain Matthew.

After the sisters drove away, my father would check

on us girls. If Grandma came over and wanted to see us, Larry followed his instructions, telling her that the girls were down for a nap. Grandma would peek in at us anyway. When she found us soaking in soiled diapers, she would bring us out to the living room to change our diapers and discover the open sores and burns from the constant presence of urine. My father and Grandmother would clean us up and put us back in the room before my mother returned home.

When my mother came home, she would always create a fight with my father over Danielle and I. He didn't pay any attention at the time, but my mother would put a string across the doorway of our room before leaving the house. If she discovered the string had been disrupted when she returned, she knew my father had been in our room. She would then accuse him of having sex with his daughters and the two of them would shout at each other for hours.

Claiming my father was physically abusing her; my mother would again and again call her father and brother to come over to protect her. My father never physically touched her, but she always elaborated on the story for her own benefit. The police would come and take my father away to jail once again. Episodes like this continued throughout their marriage; each time my mother had the upper hand. No one seemed to be listening to my father as he tried to explain the situation he was faced with.

At work one day, my father received a phone call from my mother, who was frantically screaming that the house was on fire. He told her to call the fire department and then he would rush home to help. When he got home, he found that she had once again concocted another story for attention.

If my father's parents got involved in any of these false emergencies, my mother would yell at them to mind their own business and to go home.

With my father away at work, my mother could devise new punishment and torture for us girls. I can still remember the barbaric way my mother potty trained me. My mother would strap my arms to the arms of the potty chair, my legs to the potty-chair legs, for hours each day. To force me to urinate, she would insert a syringe of water into my vagina, thinking to herself that the syringe of water would force me to urinate and then she could remove me from the potty chair. Unfortunately for me, this method was not successful, forcing me to be tied up on the potty chair for endless hours.

My paternal Aunt Jennifer happened to come over one day to visit with my mother. It happened to be one of the days I was strapped to the potty chair. My Aunt Jennifer could tell by the expression on my face that I needed to be rescued. Trying to reason with my mother while offering other potty training suggestions, my mother became defensive and insisted that her sister-in-law mind her own business. She angrily told her, "I will tend to my children my way."

My father had almost given up on seeking help for his beleaguered children when he decided to visit the county's social services department. When he met with a social worker and told them about my mother's abusive behavior, they asked him how he knew these things if he was not actually home to see these various tortures. They thought that my father must have also been guilty of these acts because he watched and didn't stop his wife's behavior.

However, they did agree to meet with my mother for further evaluation. They decided, together with my father, that the questioning would be subtle to keep my mother in the dark regarding the real reasons for the meeting.

"Are the children a lot of work?" the social worker asked my mother. "I also have children and I know they are a lot of work and need discipline."

"Yes," my mother unsuspectingly replied, "Those two girls are nothing but trouble, and I have to keep them locked up and have to punish them all the time to get them to behave."

Although my mother's unwitting confession could have brought a lot of trouble for her, social services failed to follow up on our family crisis. They failed to look at the possibility of my mother suffering from a profound mental illness, which was preventing her from caring for her children as a normal mother would. It would take more abusive behavior from my mother and more severe situations before they would take more serious action against both of my parents.

When I was about two years old, my mother went to her doctor to complain that my sister, Danielle, and I were causing her stress. She desperately pleaded with her doctor, indicating that she needed some type of medication like sedatives to help her relax during the day. Unfamiliar with the true situation, the doctor, of course, wrote a prescription for my mother to take to her local pharmacy. Upon arriving home, she started feeding the adult sedative medication to me, since she could no longer tolerate my fussing and crying.

Within days of being force-fed adult sedatives, I slowly reverted into a coma state, losing all control of my bowel and urine movements. A few days later, when my father came home one evening from work, he approached my closet door, opened it and he saw me comatose on the floor. He could smell the powerful odor of urine and bowel movement. When he tried to get a response from my body, there was none.

Despite the seriousness of the situation, my mother lashed out at my father for showing concern for me. If my father ever opened the closet door to check on me, the end result was always an extreme verbal and physical fight with my mother. But because of my physical state my father frantically picked me up and rushed off with me to Children's Hospital in St. Louis. After an examination, the doctors soon discovered that I was suffering from some type of drug over-dose, deducing that only my caretaker, my mother, could have been the person who had been forcing drugs into my system.

I spent several weeks in the hospital recovering from this drug overdose my mother had inflicted on me. My condition was reported to social services and this time they finally stepped in and took serious action against my parents. They told my parents I would be placed in a foster home in southern Missouri for one year until they could decide whether they wanted me and could take care of me. And if they could not take care of me, social services would be placing me up for adoption.

CHAPTER FOUR

A Flight from Family

After a year had passed, social services approached my parents to decide whether I would return home or if they would agree to have my new family adopt me. My mother insisted that I be returned to her, as she was the one who "borned" me, not my foster mother.

Upon my return, my father's two sisters and their families, along with my grandparents, came over to celebrate and welcome me home. My Aunt Jennifer bought me a snuggly teddy bear. Aunt Jennifer and the other relatives were impressed with the length my hair had grown during the year I was away.

I remember standing there, so small and innocent but scared and quiet with my Aunt Jennifer in a room away from the other relatives. My Aunt, on bended knees, gave me a searching look and hugged me. I looked at her with a stare of unease about the future.

My mother couldn't handle all of the attention I had gotten from my relatives at my welcome home party. She had her own remedy for the situation and the following day took the scissors to chop off all of my admired hair. When my father came home from work at the end of the day, he was once again mystified and shocked that his wife had done something so senseless again.

While I had been in foster care, my mother had had another child, my brother, Mark, who was born in April 1964. My father felt somewhat relieved when Mark was born. He knew my mother would cherish Mark and not harm him as she did their daughters.

Not long after I returned home, my parents moved

to their second home in St. Louis. The situation for Danielle and I did not improve. My brothers, Matthew and Mark had a bedroom upstairs next to my parents, while Danielle and I shared a room in an unfinished basement with hard, cold cement floors. We slept on small mattresses that lay side by side on the cement floor.

Danielle and I were not allowed to eat with Matthew, Mark and our parents at the family dining table on the main level. Our food was delivered to us at the bottom of the basement stairs, and my mother would screech for us to come and get our plates. We would take our plates and go sit in a corner of the basement to quietly eat our meal.

Many times over the years I asked myself why my father allowed this treatment to continue. Why didn't he stop the pain? How could he watch his daughters being tortured? I don't believe I will ever come up with a satisfactory answer.

As we grew older, my sister and I had developed our own ways to cope with our mother. Around five or younger, I would shrink and withdraw at the sight of my mother, but Danielle became rebellious.

By this time I had learned how to hold my urine and bowels for many hours. I didn't want to tell my mother I had to go to the bathroom strictly out of fear of what would happen to me. Both Danielle and I quickly learned that when we asked our mother to go potty, our request would result in a serious beating from her. It was an inconvenience for her to deal with our needs because they interfered with her own consuming need for attention. When we could not longer hold it, we would both go potty in our panties.

With her violent temper, my mother would tear off our panties and forcefully smear our feces and urine on each of our faces. Then she would sit us both down in front of an old stainless steel fan so that it would dry on our faces. She would always say, "Now that will teach you two girls not to go potty in your pants."

Sometimes when Danielle had to go to the bathroom, she would go in her pants and then take her waste and put it in a hole in the old plastered basement wall. When Mother found Danielle's waste shoved into a hole in the wall, she would punish both of us by placing us naked over the floor drain in the freezing basement. Even in the middle of winter, she would spray us down with the ice-cold water from a hose.

Water was a torture device in the summer as well. One hot summer day, mother brought me outside and put me in Matthew's plastic kiddy pool in the backyard. Even though I was small, she kept encouraging Matthew to dunk me underwater. Years later when my father brought me to visit our earlier homes in St. Louis, we met one of our next door neighbors, who still lived there. The neighbor, a retired policeman, told us he remembered seeing and hearing my mother encourage my brother to push me under the water and to continue to hold my head beneath the water. The neighbor remembered my mother screaming in her loud voice, "Do it again, Matthew, Debra is just a baby, she's just a crybaby." He never explained why he watched and listened in disbelief but never stepped in to stop the situation.

The yard was another source of pain if Danielle or I were "misbehaving" in my mother's eyes. Mother would pull a supple, stinging branch off a so-called "switching tree" and beat us with it, producing blistering welts all over our bodies.

Holidays supplied no relief from Mother's punishments for my sister and I. She would put us in pretty matching dresses, fix our hair just so and we would gather with my father's family at Grandma and Grandpa's house. My mother would put on a facade, but pictures are worth a thousand words. Fear cannot be hidden from a camera. When I look back at those Christmas photos at our grandparents', I can see and remember the pain and panic in those little eyes of mine as I stared with fear at my mother.

Our brothers and cousins played together throughout the day, and the adults celebrated the season, but my mother would not allow Danielle and I to play with the other children. When relatives asked why we had to sit in the corner and not play with the other children, Mother's continual response was, "They are being punished." When the other children were allowed to have cookies, Danielle and I were denied; we were being punished.

I remember a time when my mother took a trip by herself to Arizona, where her parents had just moved. She left us children with our father. When we took her down to the bus station and she stepped onto the Greyhound bus, I was so relieved. I was free. For a while, I could let go of the fear of my mother; there would be no torment from my mother. I could come out of my then five-year-old shell and have a taste of life that wasn't painful and frightful and didn't force me into my protective fetal position.

My father was freed to take his children out to buy us new tennis shoes and then would take us to a very large park in St. Louis where we could run up and down the hills of grass. The park was beautiful, green grass everywhere and blossoming trees blowing in the summer's warm breeze. I remember the wonderful feelings that came over me as I ran, laughed and played with my brothers and sister. We rolled down the grassy hills, giggling at each other all the way down. This memory was the happiest moment of my childhood.

I also recall a time when my father took us for an exciting ride in a small prop plane. We flew over the city and countryside surrounding St. Louis. I remember looking down on the fields of crops, so far below that they looked like a patchwork quilt.

That happiness was short-lived, and I remember very well the feeling of fear in the pit of my stomach when we went to the bus station to pick up Mother. Fear soon consumed me all over again; Mother was back.

Even during family outings, fear never left my body. On excursions to the outdoor movie theater, my mother would drive the white Volkswagen van. My father rode in the passenger seat holding Matthew and Mark, while Danielle and I would have to sit in the far back of the van on the floor.

Once Danielle made the mistake of standing up to tell Mother that she had to go potty. Mother immediately accelerated the speed of the van and then slammed on the brakes, throwing Danielle into the dashboard. "That will teach you to hold it," Mother screamed at Danielle. When we arrived at the outdoor theater, Danielle and I were not allowed to watch the movie; we were being punished and had to lie down in the back of the van and cover our eyes. Father got popcorn and treats for the four of them in the front, but my sister and I got none.

With a fourth child, Mother was now very emotionally and physically overloaded with the responsibility of motherhood. She decided to go to work to get away from her four children. Father encouraged her to work, since she would not be torturing her daughters if she were not with them.

Even though she weighed 250 pounds, Mother believed in her mind she could be an entertainer and she decided to become a go-go dancer at a local bar. My father told me that on many nights she would never come home after the bar closed. My father soon realized that he had lost his desire for intimacy with his wife. She was less interested in him as well and was off searching for a new man to notice her and give her the attention she was craving from my father.

One very early Sunday morning when he discovered Mother had never returned home from working the night before, my father and his brother-in-law decided to go find her. When they arrived at the bar where my mother danced, they saw the owner's white station wagon still parked out front. When they knocked on the door, a large Italian man asking them what they wanted unpleasantly greeted them. "Is Jayne here?" they asked. The Italian man told them she was inside, but my father and uncle decided not to pursue the matter and drove away. To my father it was apparent that my mother was now sleeping around.

It wasn't long before my mother approached my father with the news that she was expecting their fifth child. Although my father was amazed because he knew they hadn't had intimate relations for some time, he didn't dispute my mother's news. Even though he knew this was not his child, he decided to treat the upcoming child as his own.

Mother gave birth to Doreen, her third daughter, in May 1966. Ironically, though, there would be no torture for Doreen. Mother pushed this new baby girl onto my father and abruptly insisted that he play with and entertain their new daughter. Her persistent drive to push Doreen on my father convinced him this baby girl was truly not his.

Chapter Five

The Arizona Move

As my parents' marriage began to break apart, they would have frightful, screaming fights. We four children would run to the farthest corner in the living room and huddle close together to watch and listen. My fear forced my little hands over my ears, and I would squeeze my eyes tightly shut to block out seeing and hearing their confrontation.

My heavyset mother was a domineering female and seemed even more so in the eyes of her very young children. In contrast, my father seemed very tall and slender.

I remember a particular, full-blown verbal and physical fight when my father was wearing a white, tattered tee shirt. The incident stands out in my mind because of the strange location. We were on vacation, staying in a cabin in the Ozark Mountains. My mother, screeching in her high-pitched voice, violently pushed my father into an old black potbelly stove in the middle of the room. We children huddled into a corner to watch.

After returning home from one of her visits to Arizona, Mother told Father she wanted a divorce. After all the years of struggle to help Jayne and trying to stop the abuse directed at his daughters, my father gave up and granted her a divorce. He was full of anguish from the thought of losing his five children, knowing that she would take them and move to Arizona to live by her parents. We were being ripped out of his life and there was a chance that he would never see us again.

My father granted my mother a divorce in July of 1967. When I reconnected with my father twenty years later, as a grown woman, he gave me his reasons for letting Jayne go as well as some insight into my mother's emotional trauma that she carried from her own childhood.

He said that one evening as they were in bed, my mother had dropped into a relaxed state, almost asleep, when she began to mumble, unaware that he was listening.

She was describing a time when she was a young girl of five or six and she was in the woods with her little girlfriend. While the girls were playing, her friend's father approached them. At first he asked if he could play with the girls and soon began asking the girls to participate in sexual play with him. As the situation exploded, the father began sexually fondling both girls.

As my father listened to my mother describe this horrible situation, he concluded that his wife was so traumatized by this event that in her mind she believed no father and daughter could be in the same room together without the father wanting to have sex with his daughter. He wondered if the years of abuse my mother heaped upon her daughters were the result of her own childhood experiences. Jayne's emotionally disturbed childhood might be continuing with her own daughters, her family and her husband.

With these thoughts haunting my father, he believed that by granting her the divorce and letting the children go, she just might stop the abuse against Danielle and me.

As my mother packed the white Volkswagen van for the long trip to Arizona, she yelled at us children to climb up in the van that had boxes and mattresses stuffed within twelve inches of the ceiling. Obeying our mother's orders, we climbed up into the van and lay flat on the mattresses.

Mark, my youngest brother, was three, with snow-white blond hair at the time. He was somewhat of a pudgy little boy. At seven, Matthew, my older brother, was slender with dark brown hair. Danielle, my five-year-old sister, was blonde and also pudgy. Doreen, my baby sister, was a year old and had dark brown curly hair and a round plump face. At six years old, I was tiny and slender and had dark brown hair.

My father said goodbye to each of us but when he

approached his youngest son, my mother screeched to Mark, "Spit on your daddy, he is no good!"

As Mother demanded, Mark spit on my father and then raced to climb up into the van with the rest of us. Tears streamed down my father's cheeks as his children and his former wife drove away.

CHAPTER SIX

The "Ranch"

Arriving in Arizona from St. Louis, my mother was greeted by her parents and her new male friend she had been seeing during her previous trips to Arizona. In his sixties, Harold was a retired Army Lieutenant Colonel; he and my mother were starting a new life together with her five children.

Our new home was in the Palo Verde desert of Arizona, fifty miles west of Phoenix, where neighbors were not to be found for miles. My mother and Frank moved into a mobile home on a ten-acre piece of land. Surrounding the perimeter of the ten acre lot, Harold had built up layers and layers of huge dual tractor tires that would serve as a barrier wall against intruders. They decided they wanted to raise horses and dogs, even though the property had no running water and they would have to haul in barrels and barrels of water for the animals as well as for their own use.

With only the small mobile home, there wasn't room for five children and two adults. Only Doreen, our year-old sister, lived with Mother and Harold inside the trailer. Matthew built a tin shed for Mark and himself. Danielle and I had one army blanket and we lived in an old blue, broken down van in the far backyard away from the trailer.

Allergic to wool, I broke out in hives from the only cover I had at nighttime. We had our shoes taken away from us, as they thought it would prevent us from running away. Our daily food supply was dried out dog food, dried out bread and water from the barrels that fed the horses and dogs.

Each morning at the crack of dawn the four oldest

children (Doreen stayed in the trailer because she was a baby) would have to rush outside and in an orderly army fashion to salute Harold. As our commander, he would slowly walk by each of us, shoulders back in an authoritarian posture, his hands folded behind him. If any of us would twitch, he would grab us by the hair at the back of our heads, lift us straight into the air, kick us and then drop us to the ground. We would then have to get up and salute him again and remain there for hours as punishment.

Harold owned many army guns that he would use to march around the grounds daily, threatening us children with the barrel to our heads. We were his prisoners, ordered to work every day picking up stones and brush. If we didn't obey his orders, we would get our next breath beat out of us. He would strike fear in us and find laughter in our little traumatized faces.

As the desert sun beat down on our bodies, we each carried pails to pick up all of the rocks and debris that lay on the ground. When the sun reached its highest desert temperatures of 120 degrees, Frank would force Danielle and I to walk barefooted across large sheets of tin on the desert ground.

Our new situation was almost worse than it had been with our father in St. Louis.

By this age, I was very aware that something was wrong with my life. Some awareness within was continually telling me that what was happening to us was not how other little kids lived. I had known nothing but the hell I was born into. I was living a life of darkness and could feel nothing else. But something deep within me knew there was something better for me and that I would survive my mother's hatred for me. I somehow knew that my mother could beat me, could physically and emotionally torment me, but she would NEVER take away my will to survive.

I always felt like Danielle's caretaker. Because I was the older sister by eleven months, I took on the responsibility of caring for my sister, and I always told her I would take care of her. Danielle and I were always alone together in the van at night. We talked and made up our own games and songs in our heads since we had no toys. We did have a small portable radio to listen to and we would sing and dance by ourselves when everyone else was sleeping. We would sit up in the van and whisper and dream about another world and what it would be like. At nighttime, when stars filled the desert sky, we found our only peace. We gave each other strength to go on; we held each other to relieve our fear of what would happen each new day.

I began creating ideas of how Danielle and I could run away. I talked about the plans in detail, telling her we would leave in the middle of the night and run as fast as we could to the neighbors far up the road to tell them what Harold and our mother were doing to us. I knew if we could just tell someone what they were doing, then we would be safe.

One night I decided we were going to really run away and told Danielle every detail of my plan so she would follow along with me. After everyone was sleeping, we sneaked out of the van and lit a fire underneath the trailer where Mother and Harold were sleeping. Then we ran as fast as we could up the gravel road leading to a faraway neighbor, who lived in a big white house. Of course the plan was genius for a six-year-old to conceive. I knew that they would wake from the fire and struggle to get water from the barrels to put the fire out, which would keep them occupied while Danielle and I were running down the road to get help.

As we ran, I remember so vividly telling Danielle, "Don't look back, just keep running, and run as fast as you can, we have to get to the neighbors to get help." As our young little legs pumped as fast as they could go, we turned to look back and we saw Mother and Harold chasing us.

We attempted our escape several times, but we were caught every time and brought back to the "ranch," as they called it, and beat to the point where we could no longer stand on our own legs. I remember thinking after several runaway attempts that we should have emptied all the heavy barrels of water before we lit the fire. Then perhaps we could have escaped.

Harold always had the same reaction. He would grab us by the hair on the back of our heads, lift us into mid-air, kick the breath out of us and then drop us to the desert ground.

Despite the punishment, running away became quite frequent, causing serious worries for Harold. He was furious at us, afraid that someone would find out there were five children on the property and we girls, who were old enough, did not attend school. What if someone discovered Harold was guilty of child torture, imprisonment?

Even though Harold was the slave master, my mother didn't let up on torturing us with her games. On a hot desert day, she decided to have Danielle and I scrub the bathtub in her trailer. She came out to the van, grabbed both of us girls by the back of our hair and dragged us into the trailer. We cried and stumbled as we made our way to the trailer, where she made us squat side-by-side in front of the tub. Since there was no running water, she had to pour water into the tub.

To ensure that we began scrubbing without dawdling, she used an electric cattle prod on us. Because we were wet from the scrubbing, the electrifying zaps from the prod were extremely painful and traumatizing. We were forced to do as she demanded; if we rebelled, there would be more excruciating punishment.

As part of our daily torment, our mother took us

outside by the back of the hair, threw us to the ground like animals, and screamed for us to lay flat on our backs on the hot sandy ground. Without panties on and forced by the cattle prod to spread our little legs apart as far as we could, she poured a hot pepper powder spice into our vaginas. The burning sensation was indescribably extreme, but our screaming only intensified her reactions. The more we screamed and cried for her to stop, the more torture we received.

To this day I still do not fully understand why my mother played such sick mental games. Perhaps in some sexually ill way she believed that by destroying our genitals she was destroying a part of her female side she could not cope with. Was she trying to destroy in us something that was destroyed for her in her own childhood?

On occasion the boys would get Oreo cookies as a treat, but Danielle and I would have to stand by and watch them enjoy their cookies. I remember many times that Danielle and I were forced with the cattle prod to get down on the ground on our hands and knees like a dog and forced to eat horse manure while the boys were eating their cookies. I distinctly recall watching Mark, my three-year old brother with his snow-white hair, eating cookies and laughing while Danielle and I were eating our horse manure.

Ever since we had lived in the basement of our St. Louis home, Danielle and I had always had a fear of telling our mother we had to go to the bathroom. We still continued to hold our urine and bowels to prevent more torture. Eventually both of us would go in our panties and the punishment that resulted was even more shameful then in previous years. Again, my mother would take the feces from our panties and spread it on each of our faces. She would sit us down in front of an old fan so that our excrement would dry to our faces, but now we had to do this in front of our brothers. As Matthew and Mark stood by and watched, both Harold and Mother chanted, laughed and made freaks out of Danielle and myself in front of our brothers.

Both Harold and my mother always seemed to find our torture grossly comical and amusing, even though we were only five and six years old.

As she had done in St. Louis, my mother encouraged Matthew to participate in our dreadful punishments. She had even taught Matthew how to use the cattle prod on us. I also remember Matthew taking a normal kitchen fork and holding it over the gas burner in the trailer and then laying it on my leg to burn a fork imprint. Matthew, however, had to do as he was told, or Harold would also punish him. If any of us (excluding Doreen) did not do as Harold or Mother ordered, we were all subject to punishment.

Harold finally reached a point where he would tease and torment the boys as well. When my mother would scream at him to stop, Harold would give her the same treatment. He would actually punish her for defending the boys. He would hit, slap and yell at her as well. The more she protested over her sons, the worse he got. As Matthew and Mark grew older, Harold would antagonize the boys and the three of them would end up in physical fights. Matthew and Mark would have to defend themselves physically against the strikes and beatings from Harold. Because they were boys, they were a lot braver than us girls. It was ordinary for Harold to threaten the boys with his guns. Eventually all of us children feared for our lives when it came to Harold. Would we be killed or ever survive this horrible fate?

Our oldest brother, Matthew, did go to school. Matthew was enrolled in school as Harold and my mother believed it was safe to send him because he had no beating marks, bruises or injuries to his body that others could see and question him regarding his home life. Matthew's home life was much different from the lives of us girls. Matthew was viewed by Mother as a special child and she always went out of her way to make sure he was treated as such. Harold was well aware that Matthew had no reason to "tell" as opposed to my sister and me.

Danielle and I were old enough to be attending school, but because of our bodily injuries and our constant attempts to run away, Harold did not want to take the chance of letting us go to school and telling the authorities what was going on at the ranch.

A bus came out to the ranch every school day to pick up Matthew. Harold threatened Matthew daily as he waited to get on the school bus in the morning. Harold ordered Matthew to keep his mouth shut and never to invite friends over after school or he would be beaten.

My mother smoked cigarettes and would use them as another way to torment Danielle and I by putting them out on our bodies. I grew up hating tomato juice because another game of Mother's was to give each of us a quart container of tomato juice and force each of us to guzzle it down within minutes in front of her. If we didn't do it within her time limit, we were tortured with the cattle prod.

It also wasn't out of the ordinary for our mother to take her finger, wrap it around a section of our hair and pull out chunks of it at a time. It was another sick game for our mother to let us know that we were unwanted children.

As a child I used to wonder what was wrong with me. Why didn't my mother love me? Why was she constantly hurting me? What did I do wrong? She had a new man in her life but he was also torturing me and she did nothing to stop him. Instead, she helped him.

I remember my mother bringing home two identical

see through, sheer dresses. The dresses were mint green with tiny white polka dots. She made Danielle and I wear them when we were in public. I remember a family outing when we were forced to wear these see-through dresses. Just before we kids loaded up in the station wagon, Matthew and Mark laughed at Danielle and me standing at the bottom of the steps of the trailer with our new dresses on.

We traveled in the station wagon to a church located in the red caverns of Arizona. Trips such as this were uncommon for our family. It was a temporary urge for my mother to dress up the girls and take the family to a public place to display her perfect family image. In her mind she wanted others to view her family's outward appearance. Others were not allowed to visit the ranch, as we were hidden away when we were not working for Harold, so my mother wanted to take us out of our environment to have others see her family as the ideal family, therefore there was no dysfunction in her mind.

Danielle and I were extremely humiliated in our sheer dresses. I felt exposed and naked in front of everyone. It seemed to me that my mother would encourage others to look at us like we were some kind of freak of nature.

By this time Danielle and I were causing lots of trouble for Harold and my mother because we had made several attempts to run away. It was then that Harold told Mother she would have to get rid of us girls. There had been times when Danielle and I managed to get off the ranch, and authorities would have to bring us back home. In the end when the local police found us and took us back to the ranch, they began asking Harold and my mother detailed questions. Harold felt threatened as he was well aware that if the authorities asked too many questions and snooped around the ranch, he and my mother would be exposed and the boys would also be removed from the ranch. Harold needed the boys to work on the ranch, watering the horses and dogs and building sheds. Harold insisted that we small weak girls were not hard workers, so we were useless to him.

After thirteen months of living on the ranch, my mother gave birth to Jeff, Harold's first son. When she came home from the hospital with Jeff in her arms, she took Jeff into the trailer, leaving Danielle

Memories

This is the vehicle my Mother Jayne and Step Father Harold, along with our siblings, drove to Social Services and dropped off my Sister Danielle and Myself, September, 1968. The other children remained with my Mother and Step Father.

The trailer in Arizona, located on ten-acres in the middle of the desert of Arizona.

Our home in Arizona. My Sister Danielle and Myself lived in a van parked far behind the trailer. We were not allowed in the trailer.

A tin hut that my Step Father Harold built. He had surrounded the land with large tractor tires to keep out prowlers and to imprison us children so we would not run away. My brothers built small tin huts to sleep in with only old army beds without mattresses for sleeping.

The ten-acre piece of land in Arizona where we lived with our Mother Jayne and Step Father Harold.

Tires that lined the property lines to keep out the public and old army beds were a way of life for us children.

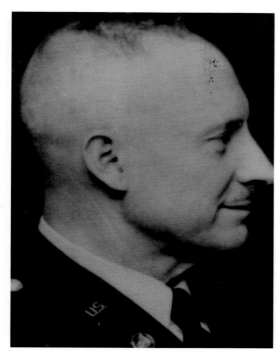

Harold, my Step Father, a retired Lieutenant Colonel from the Army.

Harold, my Step Father. My mother married him when we arrived in Arizona, 1967.

This is a Social Worker and Myself when I was being placed in a temporary Foster Home in Kansas, April 1970. This is two years after my Mother had given me up for adoption.

After returning to the "Ranch" in Arizona after 20+ years, I found my little shoes I had worn as a small child in St. Louis. A painful memory and the only tangible item left of my childhood.

and I staring up at the door. Moments later she came out of the trailer and looked at us, saying cruelly, "You two will never see this baby."

CHAPTER SEVEN

Out of This Darkness

It was one week before my September birthday in 1968 when Harold and my mother loaded all of us children in their white station wagon and off to town we went. We never saw our family again. Harold and our mother had turned us over to Social Services of Maricopa County, Arizona.

Matthew told me years later that he remembered getting back into the station wagon to return to the ranch with Harold and Mother. All of them were crying for Debra and Danielle and were asking why they took us away and where were we going? "We want to see our sisters," they cried. Even though Doreen was a toddler at the time, she remembered and talks about this fateful day. She remembered her sisters going away from the toy room and never seeing them again.

Danielle and I were both placed in a foster home in Maricopa County, with a Mexican family who had a son of eighteen. Danielle and I were frightened by this new family and wondered why we were not living with our real family. The foster parents were nice people and treated us well. Danielle and I slept in the same small bed. Danielle wet the bed and I had nightmares and I would wake up screaming and crying. I would dream that the devil was coming to get me because from birth my mother had told me repeatedly that I was part of the devil. Now I was being tortured through my dreams. I remember telling Danielle that the devil was going to come and get her because she wet the bed. Since we slept in the same bed, I was tired of sleeping on wet sheets.

On a day when our new parents were not home, our new foster brother was taking care of us. Danielle was outside playing and I was in the house. My foster brother told me to come into our parents' bedroom and lay on the bed. I did as I was told. He shut the door and pulled the blind closed on the window. He yanked all of my clothes off and raped me. I cried and was terrified. It was painful emotionally and physically. When Danielle knocked on the window from outside, he went over to the window and pulled up the blind. I looked at Danielle and cried for her to help me.

"What are you doing?" she asked. He told her to go away and leave us alone. For a brief moment I thought she could help me, but I was wrong. When he was finished, he told me it was a secret and ordered me to never tell my new mother and father.

When our foster parents came home that evening, I just stared at them with confusion. I wanted to open my mouth and speak, but no words would come out. As I wondered how I could tell them what he done to me, he glared at me from across the room as if to warn me, "Don't you tell if you know what's good for you." I was silent; my secret remained inside of me.

Our foster father was a traveling salesman and he was being relocated due to his job. As foster parents, they were instructed that they could only keep one of us girls if they moved, so I was forced to leave and go to another foster home in Maricopa County. When they separated Danielle and me, it was very traumatic for both of us. I had always believed that Danielle was my twin sister because our mother dressed us identically. Throughout our childhood we were together, watching and feeling each other's pain and comforting each other when our mother secluded us from the rest of the world. We were each other's survival, our hope, our only reason for happiness. At this point in our lives when we had to say goodbye, we were emotionally destroyed.

I remained in the custody of Maricopa County for three years, but Danielle was adopted by our original foster family. After three years of several different foster homes, social services found a family in northern Minnesota who wanted to adopt a young girl. Because I had been the one traveling from foster home to foster home, they transferred me to the family in northern Minnesota. The parents were older people who had just lost a teenage daughter in a car accident. They accepted me as their replacement daughter, and at nine-years-old, I started over once again. A new family, new surroundings. I was already confused about life and emotionally scared from the few short years I had already experienced.

My new family traveled to Arizona to pick me up at social services. On our trip back to their home I remember seeing snow for the first time. I had no idea what it was and asked if we could stop and pick some of it up. So we did. Small, almost insignificant events such as these brought joy to my life and gave me a glimpse of hope that maybe there was something better for me out there in the world.

In 1970 my biological father from St. Louis received adoption papers in the mail for Danielle and myself. Bewildered about what was going on with his daughters in Arizona, he drove to Arizona to meet with Jayne and to see his children. Since it was very early morning when he arrived at the ranch, he decided to park his car down the road and wait for sunrise before approaching the ranch. Losing track of time, he soon dozed off. Awakened suddenly, he popped up from the seat to find a rifle in his face and Harold pointing it at him.

When he rolled down his window, Harold threatened to blow his head off if he didn't leave immediately. My father desperately begged to see his children. Jayne approached the vehicle and yelled furiously at my father that she had given the girls up for adoption, and if he tried to get them in his custody, she would revoke the paperwork and re-establish her parental rights for the girls. With Harold's rifle in his face, my father felt the best move to make at this time was to start his vehicle and drive away before Harold killed him.

Returning to town to visit social services and to investigate what was going on, my father was confronted with signing the papers to release his parental rights to social services. Thinking about what was best for his daughters and about the abuse they had already suffered from Jayne, my father's best judgment was to sign the paperwork in hopes his girls would be adopted by a good family, and the abuse would end. The only hope he hung onto at this point was that perhaps someday when his daughters became adults, they would search for him. Since he felt that the adoptions might be the best for both of us, my father signed the paperwork and lost his rights to fight for his daughters.

Despite her adoption, Danielle's life experiences with her Arizona family never improved. A nudist family was raising her and to make matters worse, the father would force sex with Danielle and have her stepbrother join them. Keeping the sex secret from her new mother, she struggled with the pain and the repercussions as she approached her adolescent years.

Today Danielle is married and has one son, Carter. Carter is now married with a two-year-old daughter of his own. Danielle has been diagnosed and is currently being treated for Manic-Depression, Schizo Effective, and a "false heart." She is on several medications and unable to work. She seems to be content with her life. I often feel so sad that my sister will spend her life being dependent on drugs, psychiatrists and being confined to the four walls of her home. I look back at the childhood trauma we endured together and wonder why Danielle walked away with such extreme emotional problems and I was extremely blessed to beat our odds of survival. Today she remains in Arizona with her husband and son, her granddaughter and daughter-in-law. We stay in touch, but I find it extremely difficult to talk to her when I hear in her voice how she has been emotionally scared.

CHAPTER EIGHT

A Lost Child

I remained with a family in Crookston, Minnesota for six months before Lutheran Social Services transferred me to another family in Southern Minnesota. I was nine when I arrived at their home in August of 1970. A couple in their forties, they had one daughter they had adopted at the time of her birth in 1955 and were now looking to adopt another girl, but older than a newborn. They adopted me after the first six months of living with them.

They were quite unprepared for their new daughter's

childhood psychological luggage that was going to impact their quiet, conservative lives. Social services informed my new parents that I had been severely abused by my natural mother and the marks on my body were the results of a cattle prod that my mother used on me repeatedly. I remember my new mother commenting on the scars that remained on my body from the cattle prod, even three years later. My mother described them as red welts covering my body. Because of the trauma I had undergone as a child, social services told my new family that therapy was essential for my well-being.

When I arrived at my new family's home, I was emotionally shattered into a thousand pieces. My soul was lost. I had no identity dots to connect. My own face was a stranger to me. My reaction was to become rebellious against anyone referred to me as parents. I fought everyone internally. I refused to call any person Mom or Dad. Calling someone Mom or Dad had no meaning to me; the names had lost significance, replaced by nothing but scornful memories. I knew the new people who were asking me to call them Mom and Dad were not my natural parents, and I refused to respond to them as their child. By the age of nine, I had lived through so much evil from others that trust was not a consideration for me.

I was a lost little girl with no identity or self-esteem. I remember many nights alone in my bedroom as I stared into my mirror asking myself, "Who are you? Where do you belong? Where did you come from?" I felt that, since I had been shuffled from home to home with no family wanting me, I probably deserved to go back to my mother. I believed I deserved everything that had happened to me. Even though I knew my mother had been extremely cruel to me, I still wanted my "real" family back. As a young child, I continued to love my parents regardless of what they had done wrong. My biological family was the only tie to my own life that I could connect with. I wasn't old enough to judge my mother, I only knew how to love her.

I withdrew from family participation as I began third grade. I was desperate for love and attention and I wanted everyone to like me at school. Learning how to make friends was extremely challenging. Rejection was my major fear; it was all I knew. I was willing to do almost anything not to feel rejection again.

I learned in my elementary school years that boys really liked me. I was getting attention from them, something I had never felt before. By the sixth grade I began running around downtown with other kids, my age and older. I got involved in drinking and smoking behind the neighbor's barn while my mother was in her garden hoeing. I tried marijuana just to "fit in." I wanted to be liked by everyone but didn't care what my parents thought. Because boys accepted me when I gave sexual favors, by eleven years old I was having oral sex with boys in back of the school park. It was an exciting feeling, one that was new for me.

As I ran around with other neighborhood kids, my habits escalated into more trouble for me. At eleven I was raped for the second time. A man who would hang out with us kids at the teen center downtown was watching and observing, always from a distance. He approached me one night and asked me to go with him for a ride in his new car. I was hesitant, but my friends were chanting me on and daring me to go with him. To keep up with the peer pressure, I agreed and went with the man.

As he drove out of town, he reached over and began

fondling my vagina. I immediately got scared and reached for my door handle to jump from the vehicle. My attempt to get out of the car was unsuccessful. He grabbed me with his large hands and held onto me until he could pull the car over onto the dirt shoulder of the road. I was crying and scared.

He whispered in my ear, "Calm down, relax, everything will be okay. I am not going to hurt you, just relax."

Before I realized it, some very unusual sensations coursed through my body as he had slipped his hand down my pants. Despite the unfortunate experience, I had my first climaxing orgasm. With tears running down my cheeks, I was a terrified little girl.

When he was finished having intercourse with me, he drove me back to town and dropped me off on Main Street at the same spot where I had decided to go with him. The same friends who initially cheered me on to go with this man met me as I opened the passenger car door, stepped out of the car and onto the sidewalk. I held my head down as the tears streamed down my face, only looking up briefly at my friends with a lost and painful look on my face. As he sped off in his new car, I secretly told my friends, "He just raped me." Everyone exploded with laughter, their laughter echoed through the streets of downtown. I begged them to look at me and they would be able to tell that I was extremely upset and that something terrible had just happened to me. No one believed me. I was crushed over the lack of loyalty from my friends, who accused me of making it all up. Their rejection consumed me.

I remember always being in therapy, but I remained a troubled child, running around searching for something better than what I had already experienced. It seemed the more desperate I became, the more trouble I got into. My life had no meaning, no direction. I was trying to find love in all of the wrong ways. I was losing touch with everything around me. The road I was traveling continued to get darker and less promising for happiness. My parents were uneducated about how to deal with a child who had such a magnitude of problems. My therapist suggested a state hospital, where there was an adolescent unit with other troubled kids similar to me who were dealing with their teenage problems.

My adoptive parents, along with my social worker committed me to the adolescent unit for the next eleven months. The purpose of the program was to help me reconstruct my life, to change my behaviors and teach me a better quality of life for myself and for my new family. I became rebellious during my stay and found ways to manipulate the authorities, who were now controlling my daily activities. A girl-friend and I conspired to run away from the adolescent unit and escape to the city since we didn't want to be returned to our parents or to the state hospital.

The hospital had underground tunnels that connected the different hospital units to the entire city, but we were not successful in our escape. The authorities picked us up on the downtown streets of Rochester, and returned us to the adolescent unit, and we were put into solitary confinement for weeks as our punishment. As a rebellious eleven year old, I had to quickly learn that if I was ever going to get out of this place, I had to play their game. I had to pretend to be changing for the better and to focus on being a positive, constructive child who would listen to the adults in my life. I had to stop running away from the situations I was in and start planning constructive goals for myself. I did just that and was discharged after eleven months of structured therapy.

I wasn't home for more then three weeks before I latched onto a boy and began running around with the same group of friends who initially caused me to be sent away in the first place. We dated for two years, but he was very controlling and dominating. Two years older than me, sixteen years old, standing 5'9," tall and slender with sandy colored hair, my boyfriend Kevin and I were always alone. He was a very possessive, jealous boyfriend who did not want me to have friends, male or female, outside of our relationship.

CHAPTER NINE

A Teenage Mom

In July, I was fourteen years old when I was confirmed in our Lutheran Church. A week after confirmation I was pregnant with my first child. My mother had to tell me I was pregnant. I had no clue that being sick in the mornings was a sign of pregnancy. My parents insisted the only choice I had was to give the baby up for adoption. During the next nine months, I was tutored at home to complete my ninth grade year in junior high.

After giving birth to a six pound fourteen ounce baby

boy, the nurses brought my son to my room so that I could hold him and be with him. I was told that I could only see him once for I was being instructed to sign the adoption papers and leave him at the hospital for social services to place him in his new home.

Three days after my son was born, I left the hospital, but when I walked by the nursery, the nurses had closed the curtains so I would not see my son. My heart was broken once again, as I wanted my baby but people around me gave me no other choice than to give him up for adoption.

When my parents and I arrived home from a very long silent drive, we began discussing the possibility of going back to the hospital to bring my son home with us. We discussed in detail the lifetime responsibility that was now set before me. My parents instructed me that if we were to bring my son home, they would be the ones to help me raise him.

I was now a mother at fifteen and this new life change was extremely scary. This time I wouldn't argue with my parents, whatever they said is what I would do. We went back to the hospital that very same day and

brought my son Brian home. I did not return to junior high to complete ninth grade. I wanted to be at
home with my son. I promised my parents that I
would return to school and graduate once I became
accustomed to my new lifestyle of motherhood.

Here I was—a teenage girl raising a baby while living
with her adoptive parents. The responsibility of raising a son was beyond me; I was so unprepared. When
I turned sixteen, my high school sweetheart and the
father of my son married me. Our one-year-old son
attended our wedding.

Five years of marriage passed and I still received ongoing therapy with my social worker. We were working through my childhood emotions and memories
and managing my life as a teenage mother and wife.
As a result of therapy, I was experiencing physical
withdrawals from reality as I worked through buried
memories and pain. Lying in bed at night before falling asleep, I would get up and go down to the kitchen
on the main level of our home and curl up in a fetal
position in a dark corner and be terrified by the
thought that my mother was opening the closet door
once again. The fear of my mother's face was so in-

stilled, so vivid that I could not tell the difference between reality and the psychological trauma that I was experiencing at the time.

On the surface life was very normal for me. Behind closed doors in my therapy sessions, as my life was dismantled, I broke down and became weak. My life as a wife and mother, however, was very satisfying and rewarding for me. I enjoyed the responsibilities of caring for my children and husband. It was my internally driven mission to make the life of others around me happy and comfortable, to give them everything I never had. By the age of twenty-one, I had given birth to four sons: Brian, Shannon, Bryce and Shawn. I had been through four miscarriages and therapy was an ongoing process in my life.

As a mother, I was determined to be the opposite of how my mother behaved and how she raised my siblings and me. I was a very thriving mother when it came to loving my children and providing for their daily needs. I never struggled with my responsibilities as a mother and a caretaker for my children, as I was always determined to be 150% better mother than my own mother. My drive to be a good mother and to love my children was quite an easy task for me and was truly very natural for me. I have always had so much love to give and when I gave birth to my four sons, I was now able to explode with love, knowing that I would not be hurt in return this time.

Although I enjoyed caring for my husband in many ways, in other ways I ignored my responsibilities as a wife - the intimacy, compassion and sexual relations, the pieces that remain vital to a healthy marriage. Unfortunately for my marriage I began having affairs on my husband. I just could not get the marriage, the husband and wife relationship commitment down. The loyalty and trust that is the backbone of marriage was beyond my reality.

Because I was lacking self-love and affirmation, it was never enough for me to be fulfilled with love and attention from just one man. The attention I was receiving from men I worked with, the men I attended college with and men who noticed me when we went out was exciting and became my new intravenous drug. I had found an artificial drug that fed me all of the things I couldn't feed myself. When I arrived in Minnesota at the tender age of nine, I learned that boys liked me and their attention became my source of fulfillment. In my marriage, I was still craving the attention fix from other men. Realizing my intentions to seek out other men, my husband and I, privately and in therapy, were able to communicate, understand and cope with my dysfunctional behaviors as a wife. Extremely compassionate and forgiving, my husband was continually forgiving me for the lack of respect I had for my marriage. Even though we coped secretly, apart from the lives of our children, relatives and friends, I believe our children, more than anyone else, sensed and felt that there was trouble and tension between their parents and within their marriage.

As the mother, I organized and controlled the normal routines of work, daycare, school, grocery shopping, family events and vacations, and wanted to get more and more involved in new and different endeavors. Not that a full-time job and motherhood wasn't enough, but I desperately needed to continually search for things that would build my self-worth. I needed to pursue and get involved in as much as I could in order to avoid what was really going on inside of me. Most of my life in my twenties and thirties was spent staying very busy, keeping the outside perfect, performing and mastering everything I approached; therefore not having to face the skeletons in my closet. The childhood damage that was buried deep within my tissue was now falling off the shelf in therapy and affecting my marriage as a wife.

I pursued and graduated from college in Word Processing/Graphic Arts, Psychology major and Sociology minor. I attended a technical institute, a community college and then a university with a grade point average of 3.7 to 4.0. Much of my college drive and determination became therapeutic for I studied Psychology and Paranoid Schizophrenia, my mother's profound illness. I truly believed my career and loving and caring for my children were my destined paths. I acquired a passion for learning as a college student and I was extremely committed and determined to master a career.

CHAPTER TEN

A Frightened Adult

During twenty-six years of therapy, I attempted two suicides, and was tested and diagnosed with posttraumatic stress disorder and obsessive-compulsive behavior. The posttraumatic stress symptoms included flashbacks of my childhood, moments of uncontrollable crying and reliving the emotions and memories that were very much alive within me. The obsessive compulsive behaviors were evident in everything I did. I was a compulsive student in college. At home I was a compulsive cleaner, who made sure there was no dirt, dust or anything out of order throughout our home as I obsessively washed floors, vacuumed, constantly organized and strived to control everyone in our household. My outward appearance was always at its best. I was creating a world of "perfection" around me, which was extremely opposite of what was going on inside of me. I kept the "ugly" internal self hidden and refused to allow it to surface because I knew the pain that came from it. If no one else could see my internal pain or suffering, no one would ever suspect the pain I was really feeling from my childhood, therefore no one would ever know.

I had left work at 3:30 on a sunny afternoon, January 2, 1998. My oldest son Brian was now married and living in our family farm house 1,200 feet from our new home. Shannon, my second son, was a senior in high school, Bryce was in seventh grade, and Shawn was in sixth grade at the time. Before leaving work I handed out a letter to my boss and a few close co-workers. In it I explained how much I had enjoyed working with and establishing relationships with them, and how I had learned so much from my work experience.

I drove home from work, which was a twenty-minute

drive, and gathered every pill from my son's medication bottles that sat next to the kitchen sink. My third son was born colic and later developed epilepsy. Under doctor's supervision since the age of one, he was taking five different medications to control his grand mal and petit mal seizures. On this particular afternoon, I had dumped five bottles of his pills into a large cup and got in my car and drove to a local convenience store. I picked up a large bottle of water, got back into my car and drove out into the country. I parked in a field entrance and shut off the engine of my car. I began writing my suicide letter to my children and husband.

As I was writing, I was putting ten to fifteen pills in my palm at one time, throwing them into my mouth all at once and swallowing gulps and gulps of water to wash them down. I continued to write my letter to my family. I noticed that my handwriting was clear and concise to begin with, but then my words started to jumble and distort and were larger as I continued to write my thoughts. I felt compelled to take breaks from my writing and swallow more pills. I began writing anxiously as I could feel my system begin to react to the drugs. I became scared but pressed on, continuing to get my thoughts down quickly. Soon I had consumed all of the drugs in my cup. My reality became confused. My sense of body and mind were numb.

As I stared out the windows of my car, the sun was setting, the surroundings quickly becoming dark. I continued to write but with much difficulty. The pages grew more distorted, as I was struggling to hold the pen and write my next thought. My head was racing; my thoughts were racing. I opened the car door and stumbled out, realizing that the drugs had taken over my body. I leaned up against the car for stability. Looking up into the sky, chanting with Mother Earth, I asked to be taken.

As I walked through the plowed field, I was speaking softly to the skies above me. It was dark and I had no idea where I was or where I was going. I laid down on the rich, dark soil and spoke to the heavens. I saw visions of white cloud-like objects begin to swoop down in front of me. Fear struck me. What were these images I was seeing? Were these angels from the heavens or were they evil spirits coming to get me? At first I thought they were evil spirits. The fear of death was before me and the angels of hell were here to take me. I was desperately trying to regain the strength to run away from these spirits.

I soon discovered a sense of peace coming over me, then realized these images were angels from the heavens and they were swooping down to take me. I begged to be taken. I was ready. My body was ready to travel and to let go of my earthbound life. At that point I found peace and felt as if I were floating and my soul was preparing for this new journey. As I continued to fight the elements of my surroundings, these angels would not take me. I was ready, but they continued to swarm around me, sending me messages that this was not my time. Somehow I discovered that I needed to stand and could begin walking again. I struggled to climb through a barbed-wire fence. I could no longer see my car; I had wandered to a foreign land.

As I struggled for each next step, I came upon a farmhouse. I walked up to the house with its dimming lights and knocked softly on the door. The woman who answered the door was hesitant. I was speechless as I stared at the woman, as if to say, "Help me."

She reached out her hand and led me inside. With little energy remaining, I explained quietly that I needed help. We continued to talk quietly. When she learned my name and where I lived, she called my family.

It turned out I was ten miles from home. My husband immediately came to get me and I was admitted to St. Mary's Hospital in Rochester for urgent care and psychological evaluation. According to the doctors, I had not consumed enough pills to cause serious damage. But because of routine suicide attempts, I was admitted to the psych ward of the hospital for further evaluation. I was there for two days when I insisted on returning home. The doctor's prognosis was "depression" and "obsessive-compulsive disorder" and he instructed my family to watch me closely for future attempts such as this. Because I had not taken too many pills (heavy doses could have been fatal), I was released from the hospital without medication. The doctors insisted that I get back into therapy immediately to receive treatment for the depression.

I was thirty-six when I attempted this suicide. My

husband and children were extremely confused why I would want to take my own life. But the emotions I was experiencing that led up to this situation were obviously too overwhelming for me to handle on my own. Because I had been cheating on my husband, and in and out of affairs, I denied myself the right to any respect and dignity and the right to live. I believed that my husband deserved a "better woman," a woman he could be happy with and who would be loyal to him, a woman who loved herself, thereby loving the man she is with. I wasn't able to offer this in our relationship. I was depressed, tired and feeling extremely empty inside. I felt like a failure in my marriage, I was lousy at being a wife, and my husband did not deserve that. So I believed by committing suicide I could get myself out of the marriage, out of the lives of the family I was hurting. On the flip side, it was also my "cry for help." I wanted to stop defying the laws of marriage and stop hurting others, but didn't know how to internally and externally accomplish my goal. At the same time I was screaming for someone to help me.

Upon my return home, my husband and children watched every move I made. They felt the need to never leave me home alone, or to allow me to travel alone. This type of supervision created anxiety and added stress for all of them as they felt compelled to protect me every minute of every day. I immediately returned to therapy sessions, where my husband joined me. The psychiatrist who I was now seeing prescribed an anti-depressant drug while I underwent therapy sessions with her. With adverse reactions to Prozac, I was unable to continue taking this drug. I had never been comfortable taking mood altering drugs while in therapy since I was taught at a very early age to work through the emotions without a drug so that I was more in control of my thought processes. My way doesn't work for everyone, nor am I suggesting for you to take this path, but it was the best way for me to handle my internal mess.

CHAPTER ELEVEN

Messages from Within

Months later, May 5 to be exact, I was once again attempting to leave a world behind where I could not find inner peace. I was at home with my family watching TV in the lower level of our home. I had gotten up during a movie, gone upstairs to the kitchen and once again gathered my son's five bottles of medications and poured them into a large cup. I walked up to the master bedroom, sat on my side of the bed and swallowed a handful of pills again. As tears fell from my face, I could feel deep within me that something foreign was once again taking over my body. I had an out-of-body and out-of-mind feeling as I looked into my bedroom mirror. Staring back at me was a frightened adult, a lost soul. With every attempt to uphold my physical self, I knew something traumatic was once again taking over. Fear began to set in. This time I reached out. Screaming internally, I reached for the telephone and dialed 911 with trembling fingers.

I had only one question for the voice on the other end. What does it feel like when you are dying? As I tried to converse with the anonymous voice, I immediately realized I was pleading for help. I had put my trust in a resource I knew could save me, without being fully aware of my actions. Before I could hang up, an ambulance arrived with flashing red lights and a siren.

They had come to save me. I fled down the stairs as fast as I could to meet the rescuer at the front door before my family did so I could send them away before my family discovered what I'd done. Startled by the arrival of an ambulance, my husband and children came up from the lower level family room and met me at the front door. We stared at each other in confusion. When I opened the door and met the two paramedics face to face, I was a prisoner of denial. I pretended that I had no idea why they were there. As they explained to my husband the reason they were there, my family glared at me in astonishment.

Not wanting to admit the paramedics' allegations, I pushed my way around my husband and children and tried to close the front door behind me, but my family followed me outside. Pacing back and forth on the sidewalk, I pondered how I was going to deny my actions in front of my husband and children, but yet scream for help to the paramedics who stood in front of me. I was ashamed. Not only did I have to confess what I had done in front of everyone, but I also knew I needed medical attention or I was going to die. How was I going to get through this? As the minutes passed, I was losing the ability to speak and compose myself. I began to stumble as I paced, trying to desperately convince everyone that I was okay and that I didn't need help. Alert to the situation, the paramedics took me by my arms and escorted me to the ambulance and quickly drove me to the emergency room at a nearby hospital.

In ICU, my family was told no visitors were allowed. My heart rate was irregular as a result of the overdose, and if I were to become slightly upset, they could lose me. Consuming an overwhelming amount of prescription drugs for epilepsy actually caused my system to shut down, changing my normal breathing patterns and causing my heart rate to drop dramatically. With a tube down my throat and connected to a life support machine, my breathing was shallow. The nurses watched over me closely for the next few critical hours. Hours later, when the doctors were able to stabilize my heart rate, I was forced to drink charcoal in order to remove the drugs from my stomach. I was fighting a near death experience that was self-inflicted.

When the doctors were able to stabilize my breathing, my family was allowed to come into my private room to be at my bedside. They were still bewildered and hurt by my actions. I could not speak, but there were no words to explain. The emotional pain I experienced as I stared into the anguished eyes of my children was something I never want to experience again. Shame had overtaken and altered my appearance; it had made all of us silent.

The results of this agonizing day were much the same as after my first attempt at suicide. By this time my family felt more stress and obligation to keep me from any more attempts. Instead of recovering in a mental hospital environment, I once again returned home to the same therapy sessions as before. I now faced months of rebuilding the trust of my family and I vowed that I would never attempt to take my life again.

During the twenty years of my marriage, I wanted everything for my children. I wanted them to have everything that I had been deprived of, namely, a childhood. I showed them what love is, how to nurture. My life was devoted to their world, to family life because I wanted to give them the perfect family. The toughest challenge for me was to work through the pain and scars of my own childhood and still be the ideal mother for my children. I wanted them to have nothing but joyous memories of family life and not have to grow up with painful memories as I did.

Even in my thirties I was still searching for me; I was searching for the identity I had lost as a child. I thought the only way to find it was through external attention, sexual relations with men, partying, going to nightclubs, anywhere the spotlight could shine on me. I was screaming internally for recognition. I wanted to be noticed because I had concentrated on my own children's lives for so long that I lost my own direction and didn't know where my own life was headed. As a mother knows, your needs are always last. When those personal needs are neglected long enough, the repercussions are detrimental to the family.

My marriage was still not stable and I was becoming less and less committed to working out my personal dysfunctions as a wife. I decided to end the ongoing therapy sessions dealing with my repressed childhood emotions. I believed I could deal with whatever was going to fall off the shelf from my current situation or from my childhood by myself. After years of therapy, I was convinced I was strong enough and skilled enough to master the leftover pieces of my childhood. I had continued to work fulltime, attend college and care for my family.

Life picked up where we left off prior to my suicide attempt. With one son graduated and married, a senior in high school and two junior high students still at home, our lives were consumed with football games, band, school events and farming. I found myself wrapped up in a frantic environment and personally feeling stronger outwardly, but still felt emotionally rejected and discarded internally.

Avoiding rejection was powerful in my life. I traveled a path of abandonment and remembered what that felt like as a child. In meeting people as an adult, I did anything possible to avoid rejection and abandonment. These feelings helped set the stage for the failure of my marriage. I always suspected my husband would leave me for another woman, for I had not been loyal to him and I had demonstrated for years that I was incapable of sustaining this relationship. Therefore, I would leave first, then in my mind that would not be abandonment.

If I had the affair first, then I was protected from the pain of rejection. It was my dysfunctional thinking that sent me off into the arms of other men. My lack of loyalty to my spouse was our primary marriage problem. Looking back now with a heightened awareness, I see an oblivious woman who was desperately trying to find herself. With four children and a husband, I had a huge amount of responsibility but life was becoming too overwhelming to fully understand and cope with; I was lost.

Chapter Twelve

Time to Go

It was time for me to find my inner self. It was time for me to stop chasing whatever it was that I had been chasing for years. I didn't know how to be a loving wife. I had gone astray in my role as a wife; I had had no one to model myself after. I was convinced that this man I married at age sixteen was not "my type." I had persuaded myself that we were not meant to be together. We were too young when we married, and after years of growing apart and years of affairs there was no place for me anymore.

107

During the last and final days of our marriage, it became clear to both of us that it was time for us to go our separate ways and bring a close to this chapter of our lives. It was obvious that I was unable to fulfill my role as a wife and to remain committed to the relationship I had vowed to honor at age sixteen. We both agreed that ending this twenty-year marriage would eventually be the best for all of us. Both of us could go on with our lives without pain and disregard. With tears in his eyes and deep pain in his heart, my husband realized that he had to let me go. He could only hope I would find what I had been chasing for so many years by letting me go. I would be forced to learn and discover on my own what only I could do—heal my self.

He asked that I leave the home we had designed and built together. He was finished with the years of hurt, the tolerance and patience it took to watch his wife having multiple affairs and then forgiving her each time. The months and months of rebuilding the relationship after an affair was waning, only to discover another affair was starting up. My guilt had now eaten me up and the pain of my actions was heartbreaking to both of us.

I packed my belongings and moved out. The boys wanted to stay with their father as they could continue their lives in school and with their friends. Because they were raised on the family farm, they insisted on staying where their roots were. I drove to the big city and temporarily lived with a dear friend.

I was faced with an entirely new set of life challenges. After twenty years of marriage, the fear of being alone terrified me, and within a week I was already in the bars searching for a replacement man. A girlfriend and I went out to a dance club where we ordered drinks, laughed, danced and checked out the men. My eyes focused on a very distinguished looking man of European descent across the dance floor. I hesitated to approach him as I thought he was so attractive that he must be with a lady friend. Finally, I let down my guard and asked Tony to dance. By the end of the night we had exchanged numbers and agreed to call each other within the next few days.

In the following weeks we began dating and within three weeks I had moved in with him and his buddies. Since I was a separated and soon to be a divorced sponge and blinded by vulnerability, I would have done anything, financially or morally, for this man. Believing this relationship was heaven-sent; I gave everything for this man. I trusted and believed he was truly a businessman from Bulgaria who was in the United States on a business trip. Whatever words he spoke I heard as gospel.

As our relationship developed into a deeper level of commitment, I watched, observed and analyzed Tony's behaviors. I became a very analytical woman, who judged every aspect of the man I was now with. At first I saw hints of intolerable behavior in conversations Tony had with his friends when we were out as a group.

On a Sunday afternoon with a group of friends at a sports bar, we were enjoying a football game. After a round of shots of Jim Beam, Tony looked directly at me and commented, "See that couple at the bar? I'll bet you that I could get that woman if I wanted her. I bet that I could get her to sleep with me."

To my astonishment, I replied, "Tony, why in the world would you take your girlfriend out and make a comment like that to her? Who do you think you are?" Tony would come back with, "I was only joking." But as time went on, I became more and more aware of his desire to flirt with other women in front of me. Because I was so defensive and analytical, I refused to ignore these circumstances. Tony continued to pretend he was always joking. He would tell me to "lighten up" as his way to smooth things over.

As time passed, I thought perhaps he was right, maybe I was overreacting to his behavior. Maybe I was being too skeptical or too paranoid of his motives. Since I was the one who cheated in my marriage, I was well aware of the warning signs and habits of the "cheater." I saw my old behaviors in Tony. What he was doing was much more obvious than what I had done, he was throwing up red flags in front of me daily. I tolerated his behavior for months. Many of our arguments were based on his behavior and his disrespect for me in public and at home. But he became very skilled at comforting me when I would become upset and confront him daily on issues regarding our relationship. He wasn't going to change, he would continue to flirt with women and then would mend the repercussions with me afterward.

One year later Tony suggested that I go with him back to his country, get married and open my own business in web design in Europe. We would live near his family who he had not seen for five or six years. I believed Tony was now truly committed to a life with me, that he did love me and was serious about our relationship. I decided to cash in my retirement plan, my deferred compensation plan through my government job, and to take my divorce payoff from my ex-husband. I flew off to Bulgaria to be with Tony and his family.

When I arrived in Varna, Bulgaria, I immediately rented a newly remodeled ninth floor apartment overlooking the Black Sea. I quickly hired a private tutor to learn the Bulgarian language and set out to market my company, Web Pro Inc., a web-design and computer repair company. Making a substantial financial investment upfront, I purchased office space, computer equipment, and supplies and began interviewing and hiring employees. I traveled to Sofia, the capital of Bulgaria, which was an eight to ten hour drive from Varna, and researched and marketed my business in Varna. I met with the president and vice-president of major wine manufacturing distributors, major franchise clothing stores for women, and hotels, casinos and resorts to establish a business relationship with these local business owners.

Soon my office was established, employees were hired and I was managing, designing and marketing my business. I instantly became a business savvy woman who had a clear and logical understanding of how to take control and run a successful business.

My private life in Tony's homeland was about to take a different direction, a direction I was not prepared for. Tony was 5'5" tall, with thick, short black hair and a slightly dark tone to his skin, always reminding me of an ideal golden brown tan. An only child, he had been raised by his grandmother.

His aunt and uncle, grandmother and friends were absolutely the most humble people I had ever met. These warm and hospitable people were extremely kind and overly generous, and I grew to care very deeply for them. I became extraordinarily close with his niece, Nina, and she became my buddy. We shopped and had lunch together, spent the weekends together and had many girl talks. Nina spoke very highly of Tony, stressing that he absolutely loved me, and that she could see in his eyes that he was happy with me.

His behavior, however, hadn't changed. Once again I saw him continually flirting, believing he was God's gift to women. I watched as our relationship took a turn for the worse; I was especially cautious since I was in a foreign country, unaware of the laws and my rights as a woman.

One weekend Tony left to visit his grandmother and his daughter. I needed to stay and work in the office and stayed home. When I visited with his aunt and uncle, I discovered that Tony had been cheating on me all along. I also found out he was swindling me out of thousands of dollars from my savings account and was stealing money and equipment from my business. Since I was extremely caught up in running my successful business and oblivious to what was going on at home or in our relationship, Tony believed that he could and would get away with his behavior.

As we partied in the bars of Varna almost nightly, Tony continued his flirting. He would provocatively dance with women on the dance floor and throw hundred dollar bills to the bartender for a round of shots for the house. He became much more aggressive with me, insisting that I get out on the dance floor and join the party. Many nights I simply was not in the mood and only wanted to watch, not participate. I wasn't accustomed to getting up on tabletops and dancing with all the women in the bar. The traditions and behavior in these bars were shocking compared to what I was accustomed to in the States.

After months of the bars and following a local band night after night, Tony began to beat me when we went out. One night we had gone out to dinner with two close friends, two members of the band we followed. We went to a bar within walking distance of our apartment, on the beaches of the Black Sea.

I was somewhat reserved that night since I wasn't feeling up to the all night drinking, dancing and getting crazy. I sat with our friends, chatted and watched Tony down shot after shot of alcohol and dance until the soles of his shoes were smoking.

By 2:00 a.m., he was drunk but the bar was still hopping with other drunks on the dance floor. Tony came over to our table where three of us were quietly talking. He grabbed my arm and insisted that I join him on the dance floor with his girlfriends. In a soft voice, I refused him. After numerous refusals, Tony was extremely angry and grabbed me by my hair and led me across the dance floor, out the back door of the bar and to the sidewalk in front of the restrooms.

First he slapped the side of my head, then whacked the other side. My left contact lens flew out onto the ground. "Please Tony, don't do this, please stop!" I begged him as I bent down to search for my contact. Before I could stand back up, Tony punched me in the gut, and repeated numerous, very powerful slaps to my head. I fell to the ground from the assault but he wasn't done. He pulled me from the ground and started hitting me again. I begged and prayed I would survive this beating. During one of his slaps, I got a quick glimpse of our two friends in the distance watching Tony beat me. For a split second I thought that they would stop him, but they returned to the bar without helping me.

When Tony felt he'd done enough teaching me not

to mess with him, he ordered me up off the ground, to clean and straighten myself up and get back into the bar and sit with our friends. I was ordered not to say a word, even though I had seen them observing. We walked back into the bar, Tony's hand tightly gripping my arm so that I would not run away from him.

I wanted to run and get back to our apartment and lock him out. Sitting across from our friends, I wanted to cry out loud and ask them why they didn't help me. I was not to speak a word of what just happened as Tony sat beside me acting as if nothing had happened.

Tony walked away and approached the bar for another shot for himself. While he was away, my male friend looked at me and said, "It will be alright, don't worry about this." Somehow he thought his words would make me feel temporarily better, but they only made me cry. The mood of the night dwindled into silence.

Tony was a typical physical woman abuser who pretended to apologize and repeatedly told me he loved me and would never do it again. As I was well aware of physical abuse and its aftermath, I knew I had to get out of the relationship as soon as possible. I wanted no part of his life and began to go over plans in my head of how I was to escape this relationship and country. I lay in bed at night, crying myself to sleep, praying for my rescue until I fell asleep. I begged the Lord for strength and guidance. I needed angels sent my way to protect me and return me home to America safely. I feared for my life. If Tony could get away with beating me in a local bar, in his country, and the authorities did nothing to protect me, I knew I was in way over my head. My tutor, when I first came to Bulgaria, told me in very clear English that in Bulgaria women have no rights. The police would only laugh if a woman showed up at the police station begging for help. Now what was I going to do? How was I going to get myself out of this country?

Tony began threatening me that he would force me into prostitution or would take me out into the country and have someone finish me off if I left him. As I cried myself to sleep at night, I prayed and prayed. My emotional choices had once again caused me to go down the wrong path. I prayed to have my sons rescue me from this situation, to get me back home alive and safe. I felt my children were my only strength, they would be my angels.

Privately, I went to James, my business partner, and shared with him what Tony had done to me and how he was threatening me. I begged him to take me to the travel agency and help me arrange for the quickest flight out of Varna. Tony was planning to be out of town again, so this was my only chance at escape. My tutor came to my apartment and helped me pack an essential suitcase and then we went to her apartment. The next day James and I purchased my airline ticket.

I was leaving my relationship with Tony, my business, and my Bulgarian friends. After eighteen hours of travel, I arrived at the Minneapolis, Minnesota airport on October 18, 1999. My children, who had not seen me for two years, greeted me. The only communication we had had while I was out of the country was e-mail and sporadic phone calls. I was blessed and protected by my angels. I had arrived safely back in America.

Unfortunately, my Bulgarian experience not only

tested my emotional strength, but stripped me from twenty plus years of financial stability. I lost over $100,000 in cash, computer hardware and software equipment, and a 1994 Mitsubishi VR4 red sports car and years of personal collectibles that I was forced to leave in Bulgaria.

CHAPTER THIRTEEN

A Dare for Dignity

When I returned, I decided I wanted to live in Minneapolis. I had loved living there prior to going to Bulgaria and this was where I wanted to start over. My poor judgment in Tony had caused me to lose everything financial and material; I was once again lost with no direction. I had no furniture, no way to live alone and provide for myself. I had to rely on friends once again to start over. Not only was I emotionally destroyed from my European experience, but I had nothing to call my own.

I quickly found a place with dear friends, and got myself a management job in a restaurant. At this point I knew that baby steps were all I could do to rebuild my life. I felt badly about imposing on a family, who had their own lives, by taking a bedroom in their home, but I had no other choice at that time. I worked long hours and was determined to pick up the pieces and rebuild my life. With a strong mindset, I set high standards for myself and I slowly reconstructed my life.

This time I allowed myself to heal emotionally before jumping into the next relationship. I kept myself busy and met new people along the way. I had small conscious goals and stayed focused or I knew I could hit rock bottom again. Trust became my worst enemy. I trusted no one. My walls went up and stayed up. I had to re-examine what it meant for me to say "yes" and what it meant for me to say "no." I had to re-evaluate my resistance and vulnerability. I had to toughen up and be aware of the cruel people in the world who feed off the weak.

After months and months of pouring myself into my career and developing new friendships with co-workers, eventually I allowed myself to go out again.

With my guard up, I felt ready to venture out and to be prepared to distinguish the evil people from the good people in the world. In the past, I had always been extremely trusting of others, too trusting. I would open myself up to anyone and everyone to gain acceptance. At this point in my life I had to sharpen my senses if I were going to survive.

On an evening when I emotionally needed to detach myself from the friends I was living with, I decided to get myself dressed up and go out alone. Their hectic lifestyle was becoming a liability for me. They had two small children, and the sounds of screaming babies were getting to be too much for me to tolerate, I needed a break.

I had never gone out alone. Scared to death of this adventure, I did just that. Face your fears, right! It felt extremely awkward and out of place for me to do this. I have always been a people person, loving the company of others. But this night something in my gut said just do it. So I did.

I met a young, quiet gentleman this night, who approached me and began talking softly to me. General questions, what is your name, where are you from. Because I was practicing my new personal powers, I found my reactions to be somewhat cold, maybe rude. I viewed this man with severe skepticism. I listened, observed and took the situation at face value. I watched as he would reach up and brush his hands through his striking blonde hair. I took mental notes as I watched his facial expressions. The two of us talked for the remainder of the evening. We seemed to have so much in common, but I was trying so hard to see if there were any warning flags.

We ended up planning a date to go to the movies the following Sunday afternoon and then grabbing a bite to eat afterwards. I met Steve at the movie theatre and we thoroughly enjoyed ourselves. He softly laid his hand on my knee during the movie. His energies were powerful, and he was so kind. Afterward, we went to an upper class sports bar and had dinner. Once again we found ourselves totally absorbed in conversation. We had so many great stories to exchange and found that the resemblance in common life experiences were the focal point of our reason for meeting and connecting. With the noisy crowd in the restaurant surrounding us, we talked about spiritual and practical topics that took us into our own secluded world.

Shortly after, Steve went on a two-week vacation to his parents' home in Cabo San Lucas, Mexico with his best friend, Randy. I continued to work and carry on with my own life, rebuilding slowly. When Steve returned from Mexico, he called me. We talked for two hours and discussed developing a serious relationship together. After we'd dated for months, Steve discovered that I was not living in a healthy environment and was compassionate enough to invite me to move in with him. Seeing me struggling and trying to rebuild my life, he wanted to help me. I took him up on his offer and moved in April 1, 2000. We both struggled with the adjustments. Steve had been living alone for four years prior to meeting me and I was still searching for where I belonged, where was my life was headed.

In the trials and errors of relationships, I had finally found my soul mate, I believe the most loving man alive. He is a man who respects me, who is not going to take advantage of my vulnerable side, a man who recognizes and respects my strengths and never questions my weaknesses. My life has changed 180 degrees. He built me up and encouraged me to start up my web design business out of our home. I became a consultant in the world of computer information technology. I became very centered and focused on my career and my new life with Steve. We laugh, discover common interests and work hard together to make sure both of us are happy.

I am now traveling a path of light. My career is doing exceptionally well. We sold Steve's town home, and rebuilt our own little sanctuary. As a hobby, Steve and I enjoyed house hunting. We talked often of building a home we could call our own. On weekends we ventured out to the new developments in the area and attended the "Parade of Homes" in our area every spring and fall. We had so much fun, we laughed, and we had serious discussions of design plans and goals for our new home. After researching and planning, we decided to build a town home, and for six months we customized, built and then moved into our new home in October 2001. We were married December 1, 2001, in our new home. After a private ceremony at 11:00 a.m., we invited family and close friends to an open house reception to share in our new beginning.

Our marriage feels so true. Both of us are poetic, exuberant and keenly insightful to the world around us. I couldn't have married a more respectful, thoughtful person. We have many blessings in our life, which includes having very gifted families and friends and nothing but love and light embracing our home.

Chapter Fourteen

Embers of the Soul

How do we really know if we are traveling our destined path? For years chasing the unknown, I stumbled many times. I repeatedly made the wrong choices, bad choices. Many times I had to pick myself up and travel down an unknown path. Faced with fear, challenge and self-doubt, how was I to make such a journey? It's like traveling down a deserted road at night, when only darkness is around you. I had blinders on and I was asked to find my way. How was I to take this journey alone? Was I alone on this journey? What tangible things could I do in my life to be a stronger individual, to be a person who relied less on those around me? How was I to believe in myself without others providing hourly affirmations that would keep me moving forward down this unfamiliar road?

I had to look at the world around me from a practical perspective and at the same time heal and repair the internal damage of my past. With everyday distractions and obstacles, I had to examine a great variety of channels. I had to reinforce my own internal strengths and remember my God-given gifts I used to survive my childhood. I have always relied on family and friends to pick me up when I have fallen from the nest. Now it is time in my life when I need to rely less on those around me and do the work set before me on my own. It's obvious to me at this point that I have survived my hellish childhood. Now I have to use those same internal strengths to survive my adult life. I have to use those gifts to heal internally and find happiness and serenity.

Of course my body is tired. I have had years of hard work and experience. My shoes are worn and the life-long tapes that played in my head over and over again have now been deleted. I have hang up on those voices. What was the sacrifice for me? What is my life like now since I created new messages? Since it was a journey that created fear, apprehension and procrastination, to describe it mildly, I had to become intimate with myself in order to repair my childhood damage. I had to clean up the inside. Wow, the thought of facing my inner self, boy is that scary! That's scary for all of us, to look inside.

Of course my outward appearance was always perfect. My hair, makeup and the way I carry myself has always been nothing short of perfection. I dress stylishly, top-notch attire, with no seam out of place. If I am perfect on the outside, no one will see through to the inside, the inner me filled with ugliness, distortion, a lack of self-esteem and self-worth and full of old pain and fear. I believed that if my outward appearance was always above the standard, then everyone would expect the inner me was the same. This philosophy made sense to me.

I created a world around me that was nothing less than perfection. My home has always been spotless, my desk at work is always orderly, and my vehicle, garage and yard are always clean. I became very intuitive, observing of others around me. I spend endless energies on detail. My children always had orderly closets, the best hip-hop wardrobes and all of the toys they ever dreamed of. Clothes were perfectly folded. Meals were chef mastered. The energy it took for me to create this flawless, orderly, detailed world has kept me almost completely occupied and distracted from the real issue, repairing the inner me. If I kept myself consumed in making all external aspects of my life perfect, then there was no time to clean up the inside, right?

Today I have forced myself to awaken. I have forced myself to examine where I came from and to acknowledge my childhood environment, which unfortunately set the stage for the remainder of my life. Our childhoods from birth to six years of age are the most impressionable years in a person's life. These are the years that will set the stage as we play out the rest of our lives. There was much darkness, no love or nurturing in my childhood. What type of an adult would I become? Was this childhood going to force me to become a deadbeat, a criminal or a person who is worthless? Even with years of therapy, where I spent many sessions crying, letting go, setting goals and trying to move on, I still found myself searching for something. What was this something? Why was this not coming to my conscious level so that I could acknowledge it and fix it? I chased this something, but it was always unclear what it was. Was it my identity? Was it my spirituality? Was it happiness?

Soul searching is a very tough process when you haven't been given the "guide to a healthier life" manual from within. I was spending most of my life avoiding and procrastinating the internal clean up job. If I ignored it, it didn't exist. If I didn't feel pain, I didn't have to face fear head on. I thought that I could lead a healthy and happy life ignoring what were the most prevalent feelings in my body, my soul.

I have grown into an adult woman who has set the highest standards and expectations for herself. I always expected myself to succeed in any adventure I took on. The fear of failure creeps in like a plague and strikes me when I least expect it. But I have learned to acknowledge the fear is present, then let it go because it's not real and stay focused on the positive energies coming from within.

CHAPTER FIFTEEN

Floating Spirits

It seems like it has taken me a long time to get to a place where I am finally focused on healing the internal me. After years of being hit over the head with a two-by-four from God, I have finally embraced his open doors with joy. I spent so much time crawling down a path because I was stubborn and believed the path I wanted to travel was the right one. I have finally stood up and have begun walking. I have been met by my angels, who are walking straight toward me, and are here to help me in the remainder of life's journey.

135

Michelle is not a stereotypical massage therapist, and it was not a coincidence that I met her. I initially went to Michelle because I had received a gift certificate for a massage from my husband. Working as a consultant in the corporate world, my contract job was negatively consuming my well-being. The aura of the managers around me projected like wind tunnels, their own hatred, negativity, depression and misery. Deceitful attitudes were swarming all around me and overpowering my own situation. As I started seeing Michelle for relaxation messages, I was making baby steps toward something larger than I could have ever imagined.

As I have always relied on my intelligence, success and professionalism to hide my inner self, I was now discovering techniques to begin healing myself. There is an energy field, a reflection of life's subtle energies within our bodies. But before I could tap into that awareness, I had plenty of work to do on myself. For years my body had been filled with large amounts of darkness, evil that was hiding out internally from childhood pain and fear. I was now faced with working harder then ever with Michelle to "throw up" or "exhale" all of these old scars before physically or emotionally feeling at peace. The auras our bodies reflect indicate our health, character, and mental activity and, of course, our emotional state. An unhealthy aura indicates the onset of disease.

My search was over and now my work had to begin. I had been searching for healing, for spiritual peace. I had been searching to uncover the existence of my true aura. Not an aura on life support tubes of negativity, self-doubt and lack of self-love. My pain and fears were now being challenged. With the help of Michelle, I am still learning to relax and meditate as a ritual part of my lifestyle. Drawing from the powerful hands of Michelle, together we are getting rid of the darkness, the pain and fear, the demons that have lived within me for too many years. How to recognize these clumps of darkness, pain and fear was my first mystery. Massaging masses in your body and working them out of your body is called CranioSacral Therapy.

CranioSacral Therapy is performed on the body using a light touch. The practitioner monitors the rhythm of the craniosacral system to detect potential restrictions and imbalances. The therapist uses a delicate, manual technique to release those problem areas and to relieve undue pressure on the brain and spinal cord. The central nervous system and body tissues are freed of restrictions by this therapy, resulting in the body releasing the emotional energies necessary to fully discharge a trauma.

Research conducted in the late 70's by Dr. John Upledger and biophysicist Zvi Karni led to the discovery that the body often retains the emotional imprints of physical trauma. These imprints, especially of intense feelings that may have occurred at the time of the injury—anger, fear, resentment—leave residues in the body in areas called "energy cysts."

Over time my body became worn down, while my body was also demanding extra energy in performing day-to-day functions. As years passed, my body became more and more stressed, losing its ability to adapt. Symptoms and dysfunction began to appear and became almost impossible to ignore.

Long-held emotions had been hiding out in my body, affecting my physical and emotional performance. I wasn't aware of the problem before working with

Michelle. With Michelle's light touch and the monitoring of my "energy cysts," we have been able to expel my darkness, pain and fear, my "energy cysts" from childhood trauma.

It has been a life changing experience that I have fully embraced with open arms. I feel like I have been reborn. I live a much more peaceful life. The old pain and fear from childhood have now left my body. I have filled the empty cavities where these energy cysts hung out with love, light and happiness. Prior to this experience, I was a chronic worrier. The energy of worry and the physical stress that consumed my body has now left my body. Contrary to my own beliefs, the healing process was much more gentle and subtle than I had ever imagined.

To me, the practice of CranioSacral Therapy is a miracle. Michelle, you are an Angel who has been sent to me after twenty-six years of psychotherapy, chiropractic care, posttraumatic stress and physical and mental dysfunction in my life. I have never felt more centered or grounded. Thank you for coming into my life, Michelle.

Chapter Sixteen

A Miracle Flight

Reaching as far back into my memory as I can, I knew long ago that I had a gift that no other had. Something greater was empowering me; therefore, I knew anything was possible, death or survival. Strength may be just one of those gifts I received at birth. If I had to make a list of gifts I have received over my lifetime, the first item I would list is an awareness of "infinity." My list goes on forever and ever and for that I have been truly blessed.

I could always see something even deeper than the conscious level of my existence. Something deeper

141

than most will ever identify during their lifetimes. Inescapably, I was and always will be God's Angel forever. He had a plan for me, as he has a plan for all of us and somehow, someway I identified with this feeling long ago. But my true gift was the ability to identify with this at a very young age. I had the sense that this trauma was wrong, that I had to tell the world so that it would go away and make my life better, even though I wasn't quite sure what better meant at the time. I always knew the tragedy that consumed my childhood would someday be my reward. Take trauma and turn it into a reward.

Recollecting the past and the paths I have traveled, it is apparent to me that I have conquered the darkest of my life tragedies, far beyond merely surviving. Even though the past has shaped my adult actions and exhausted the visions of my purpose, I have been able to shake the evil curses that have challenged my survival. My past reminds me of the struggles of self-knowledge, of self-love.

Determination has been my driving force every step of the way. The search for so many answers to my questions became a detour in my healing process. I took a vow long ago that I would set the highest standards for myself and live by those standards. If I accepted anything less then those standards, I had just set a new set of standards for myself.

I am now traveling a road never traveled. By healing from the inside out, by uncovering and letting go of old pain and fear, my eyes see more clearly; my heart's damage is now mending. In my events of healing, I have had to let go of the roadblocks of fear. No more U-turns from happiness. The drought of doubt is only our internal fight with God. I have been forced to give credit where credit is due.

My courage to travel a new path motivates me to do what I have never done before, practice and live by self-love. I will never collapse to the floor in despair and refuse to move forward. Lives have touched me, angels are celebrating, and the internal work has started for me. I have discovered an entirely new level of self-affirmation, an internal peace and balance. Pain and fear will no longer rule my being. I have been a prisoner of my past, but only I can compete against the trauma instilled, the trauma left behind. Only I can write fan letters to myself, praising my gifts and describing to myself who I really am after all.

CHAPTER SEVENTEEN

Pulling the Sword from My Heart

"If you have time to judge people, then you have no time to love them."—Mother Theresa!

I will share with you what I have learned in the painful adventure of my life. I have traveled a deserted, lonely road without the two people who were dearest to my heart. I have spent many years craving the love of both my parents, the encouragement while growing up, the support behind my dreams, the shoulder that I could lean on to shed a tear of loss.

You, my parents, were not there. The loss that I felt as a young child would set the precedence of my adult life. As I stared into the sky as a small girl, I fumbled with thoughts of both of you. Where were you? Why didn't you love me? Why were your lives not devoted to spiritually teaching your offspring the gospel of love? Why has fate separated me from my parents, my siblings, leaving me to grow up alone? What deeper purpose was out there for you leaving my side? What was to happen to my soul without you?

My soul has been terrified for too many years. I want the pain, the sense of extreme loss and the old fear to exhale from my body. I have lived as a frightened child and as a frightened adult. A sense of hell is the most accurate way to describe it. I wasn't brought here to judge you or decide what punishment you deserve to counterbalance my pain. But I do know one thing, you let the most precious gifts slip through your fingers with no desire of return. You dropped off heaven's gifts along an abandoned road as if to eliminate a piece of yourselves. You fled from a piece of your own creation.

It was hard for my small child to understand why I

was suffering, why I was feeling only emotional and physical pain. I remember simply glaring at both of you with confusion and sadness. Not only did I have to find child coping mechanisms to survive the events, but also to discover as I grew up to be this beautiful woman, that I was alone and abandoned with no love. Left with no identity, no connection to the world around me, I was lost. I was a masterpiece of your own creation who you simply walked away from. Drawing from my only source of existence, I had to explore how I was going to survive without you. What type of person was I to become? What type of person would I have turned out to be if had I been under your wings?

I am the baby bird who was forced out of the nest with a broken wing, a wing that has been broken for many years.

As a child I prayed that you would rescue me, that you would mend my wing. There was nothing more splendid in my child's life than to daydream that my daddy would rescue me. I wanted you to mend the pain of evil acts as parents. No one came, no one knocked on my door. There was nothing but silence in the realm of my head. The mirror was all I had to connect my body and mind. The reflection that stared back at me gave me no answers, just more confusion. It set the stage for self-doubt, lack of self-worth and most importantly the absence of self-love. I had nothing to rebuild. No tools, nothing but strangers called Mother and Father. Those words are empty for me. They mean nothing to me. My internal dictionary is empty. The files were deleted when you let go. I spent years with no oxygen to my soul. I was choking from the memories that swarmed in my head. You disappeared and all that was left were painful memories.

How could you? I had a mother with an extreme illness, and a passive father. Father, you had a choice to tolerate evil as it crept into your lives or to battle the odds. It was you who chose to wear the shields, to become a passive father. Willingness to save the children would only generate work for you. The face of the passive father is only the face of self-centeredness. The work of a father did not inspire you, it only disrupted your plans. Your only vision of the ending sequel was to protect yourself, not your creations. You killed the dreams of five small children by walking away and throwing away the key, the keys to your children's lives.

Denial protects you against any possibilities of having to face truth head on. If you were forced to face truth, you would have discovered you were guilty of what you already knew internally - neglect, selfishness, passiveness and self-indulgence. Your restless body could not afford to expose your own decadent or frivolous behaviors. It was simply easier for you to paint a pretty picture for yourself, while also painting an ugly image of the real wrongdoer. Instead of presenting yourself as the victim, you should have done more protecting for the sake of your children. Whether it was a conscious intention or not on your part, your pilgrims were stuck with separation. We were thrown from the nest and would spend the remainder of our lives healing the wounds, repairing our souls and finding our purpose. Without your support, the lifelong struggle has been intensified beyond anything you can see or touch.

My parents never acknowledged my child's pain. The depth of my being was damaged; the struggle of coping was the new challenge set before me on the last day you saw me. I was sent out into the world at six years old with nothing but catastrophic memories. The load that I carried was far deeper then the bump or scrape that requires a band-aid or the hug and a pat on my rump to carry on. As I was thrown from the nest, it was a point of transformation, a crossing over. You were not by my side on the path that I have traveled. I took this journey alone. I had no family to reach out and touch, to feel with me, to heal with me, to guide me. You were not there.

Mother and Father, you are both strangers in my world. I don't know who you are. I have tried to con- nect my spiritual dots back to you but my weak heart can no longer make the connection. I have gone through the loneliness, the pain and sorrow alone. I have traveled through my spiritual healing process alone. There is no place in my world for you. It is my turn to walk away and not stop and turn around to see if you are following, when you should be leading. I no longer search for my place. My search is over. There is no place in the realm of my space where you belong.

My child will always be with me. I will pamper and

love that child like no other. I will love my child like I love my own children. I will take her hand and guide her through the remainder of her life. No one being will ever bring pain to this child's heart as her parents did. She has blossomed into a beautiful middle-aged woman through the help of angels around her. I have always been strong because I knew I had to protect my child with every blast of energy in me. The life dots are now connected through my own children and the joy they bring to my world.

Chapter Eighteen

Trapped in the Past

I didn't search for my biological family until the latter part of 1984 when I was legally of age, according to the adoptee laws at the time. I had waited years for this opportunity. It was my innermost dream to search for my natural family and be reunited with everyone. Deep inside I had always prayed that we would be a family once again. When I grew up, I would bring everyone back together again. Growing up in unfamiliar surroundings for years, being shuffled from home to home like a lost piece of luggage, living with strangers who vowed they loved me, I hung onto my own internal fantasies that someday I would be reunited with my real parents and siblings.

I was a housewife with two children at home. My husband worked from home while I cared for the children. I was always involved in crafts, hobbies and creative little projects that would keep me feeling productive, artistic. In the next three years I found myself searching library records—phone books for the states of Arizona and Missouri—to find my family. I had the memory of an elephant for names and locations as a child, details that were still fresh in my mind as an adult. I made numerous phone calls to the post offices located in the Palo Verde, Arizona area, asking them if they remembered our last name or maybe the names of my siblings, by chance. I quickly learned in my search how to backtrack time in order to locate members of my family who may or may not have remained in the local vicinity of where I last lived, also referred to as the "ranch." After gathering the names of high schools in the Palo Verde area, through phone books and directory services, I placed several phone calls and had written several letters to specific individuals, who might remember our family or one of my siblings after I left in 1968.

In addition to my own hard work of tracking down my family, I also hired Search Triad, Inc. to help me locate my sister Danielle. Since we were the only two who were given up for adoption by our mother and father, I was required by law to travel to Arizona and present my case before a judge in order to get court orders to open the sealed files of our adoption. This was another method to locate Danielle. Despite my trips to the Arizona courthouse, I had prepared flyers to post in the local convenient stores, gas stations, 711s, just to name a few. With the flyers I was hoping to locate Danielle and my younger brother, Mark. I searched social security numbers by their names and death certificates just in case.

Within six months of returning home and still pursuing the search for my family, I received a phone call on a Monday evening at 8:00 p.m., from a young woman, who indicated her name was Doreen and that she believed she was my baby sister. Contacting the school systems in Arizona and the specific counties had finally paid off. The school authorities had received my letters and with that information they did remember my sister Doreen from high school. They called my sister with information that her sister Debra was searching for her and provided Doreen with my contact information. I had found one sibling with my efforts. In the two-hour conversation with my baby sister, she quickly informed me that she was also in touch with our older brother, Matthew, our mother and two step-siblings. Connecting the dots of my family was coming together after all this time. We were extremely excited talking together, although it felt bizarre. It felt as if I was talking to a stranger and then sharing memories with a sibling, minute by minute. Before we ended our phone conversation dealing with the past twenty years, we exchanged addresses and phone numbers, and Doreen provided me with the details of our brother Matthew and our mother, who were both living in Arizona, near Doreen.

The following evening, 9:00 p.m. on Tuesday, I decided to call Matthew, my older brother. It was once again a very strange and out of reality phone call. Here we were, years after our separation, discovering that our lives did go on, we did grow up, we were strangers, but yet we still had something in common, our childhood memories. It was, of course, a good feeling to once again be within telephone distance of my family. I was getting closer; we were once again connected. Matthew and I also spent two plus hours exchanging memories, thoughts, and our current lifestyles with each other. He also confirmed, as Doreen had done the previous evening, that our mother was living near Matthew and his wife. Without hesitation, Matthew encouraged me to give our mother a call. Without sharing the fear that consumed me when we talked about our mother, I was able to subdue my emotions toward our mother over the phone with Matthew. I knew before I talked to Matthew for the first time in twenty years that he was and always will be very close to our mother. And I was more than sure he was aware of my apprehension toward Mother. Time, as in weeks and months, had to pass before I could find enough courage within me to call my mother for the first time after twenty-six years.

In the meantime, organized with a well thought out plan, I was able to move forward with my family search and utilize the services of my counseling office to assist me in locating my father in St. Louis. With the help of my social worker, a few court orders and a few phone calls, we were able to locate my father, who still resided in St. Louis. My social worker at the time communicated directly by letters and then by phone with my father, arranging the reunion with his daughter, who was extremely anxious to meet him once again. After years of separation, I knew my reunion with my father was a dream come true. I had waited for this moment since the last day I saw my father's face in 1967.

I met my father for the first time in twenty-one years on my birthday weekend. As my husband and I drove the eight-hour trip from Minnesota to St. Louis, I couldn't stop talking, I was extremely nervous. The numerous crazy thoughts that ran through my mind as I tried to convince myself this was going to be a moment I had always waited for. With tears in my eyes and my hands trembling to the point that I couldn't hit the doorbell straight on, I was about to meet my biological father.

The door opened. As the storm door swung by my cheeks, a petite man with a soft-spoken voice greeted me. This was my father. Wow, what a moment this was. I was struck with shock and speechless as I stared at him. His features were as if I had been looking into a mirror and a version of myself was looking back at me. We resembled each other so much that it became scary for me to continue to stare at this stranger who I had been told was my father. I was sure he had similar confusion and fear. Our facial features were almost identical, body size and mannerisms were also very similar. I continually repeated over and over in my head as I stared at my father, "How could this stranger look just like me when I don't even know him?" I didn't know this man, but there was something unique about him that made me feel connected to him.

Soon we hugged and formally introduced ourselves to begin a weekend of hours of reminiscing, questions and memories of our earlier years. As the weekend days became shorter and shorter, I observed my father's interpretations of my childhood, his version of my mother's illness. His insights and detailed experiences were not shocking to me as I also shared with him what memories, pain and abandonment I walked away with twenty-one years before. It became obvious to me that all of us endured tremendous repercussions of my mother's inability to be a mother and wife. But as my father frantically protected his role in our family, I watched, observed and became concerned with the overwhelming guilt he had carried after all of these years. I witnessed a man, with what appeared to me as desperation, who spent every moment trying to free himself of any responsibility for our family failing. It was becoming clearer and clearer to me that he was denying in his nervous voice that he could have stopped my mother before her beatings occurred. The only man in my life as a young child, who I loved and looked up to for protection, was once again serving his own intentions. His passive attitude prevented him from helping us, I was convinced.

I no longer wondered how my mother repeatedly beat and tortured her daughters daily. I no longer wondered why someone, specifically my father, did not get her medical and psychological help. The more time I spent with my father, the more I realized that we were two extremely different individuals. After this weekend, and the years of visits that followed, I never ever wished again to be like my father. We were two very different souls. It's as if we had nothing in common anymore, if ever. Imagine meeting an old friend you haven't seen for years. You get together and catch up on old times and then say goodbye for another five to ten years. You return to your life, your daily routine and find no common ground with this old friend in your schedule. Somehow this is how my relationship with my father has evolved in the last ten years. There is nothing left. I have too many buried thoughts and emotions that I have not shared with him and choose not to in order to protect myself. His failure in saving me as an innocent child has disappointed me beyond a conscious level. I don't have time to judge my father, nor is that a part of my destiny, but I have chosen to detach from my life from his. Simply put, he had done nothing to save me then; what could he possibly have to offer me today that would be rewarding for me as an adult. Nothing.

After finding my father, I was faced with the attempt of calling my mother for the first time. I decided to call her. I was alone in my bedroom, away from my own small children.

My hands trembled as I slowly dialed her number. I heard the first ring, then the second ring. On the third ring a voice answered, "Hello." Silence before the storm.

There was a pause on my end before I could physically bring a sound from my voice. With a trembling body and a quivery voice, I replied, "Hello, Mom, this is your daughter, Debra," as I silently prayed for her acceptance and love.

"Debra, is this Debra?" my mother answered in her familiar, haunting voice. The voice was back. A buried memory of my mother's voice resurfaced immediately, it was as if it had never left my body, only hiding out in my tissues. Her reply was as striking and scary as ever was, "You are the Devil, you are a Devil's child."

The old feelings of horror returned. I was struck with the emotions of terror, disappointment, pain, sadness and failure. My mother still didn't love me after all of this time. The voice I heard was a replay of inner messages from childhood. Here I was a grown woman still searching for my mother's love and acceptance after all these years. I wanted her to miss me, to be so happy I had finally contacted her. Hearing her fiery voice and hearing her raging about me being a part of the devil, that unsettled darkness and mass of destruction came to the surface once again.

I had so many questions for my mother. I immediately became very blunt and assertive as I asked her, "Why did you give Danielle and me up for adoption? Why did you not love me? Why did I deserve your torture and punishment?"

My mother's reaction was consistent in tone and content. "Because you were evil, you and your father are both part of the Devil. You two girls were nothing but trouble."

I soon realized in this conversation that my mother was once again expressing her hatred for me. She still did not love me and still would not accept me after all those lost years. Something told me that if I didn't keep quieter about my feelings and didn't ask all of the questions going through my mind about my childhood, I might never get a chance to confront her again. I felt that this phone call would be my only opportunity to confront my mother.

I began asking more and more questions. "Why did you lock me up in a closet? Why did you torture me and cause me so much pain? Why did you not love me? I was such an adorable, innocent little girl who only wanted to be loved by her parents. I only wanted to grow up with my siblings and you took all of that away from me."

My questions were flowing so quickly that I never gave my mother a chance to answer. Her only response to my frenzied voice was, "I didn't do that to you. Who told you that? Your father put those evil ideas in your mind."

I soon realized that this conversation was going nowhere fast. I realized my mother was still a very ill person and was not in touch with reality. Her mind was so delusional that all she could do was respond with the same repetitive message that I heard as a child: "You are evil, you are part of the Devil." She did not even try to defend her actions, she just continued to yell at me, "You were a terrible child, and I had to discipline you." Her words crept throughout my body as if I were traveling back in time and hearing my mother's voice when I was a child again.

Feeling extremely frustrated with the conversation, I realized the only logical thing to do to protect my emotions was to just hang up. A big piece of me was just hoping to hear in this conversation that she would apologize and express to me how very sorry she was for everything she had done to me as a child. I wanted to hear her ask for my forgiveness and express her love for me, to hear her interest in getting to know me as an adult and to rebuild our relationship from there. I was up against my mother once again, but although my dream had instantly died when I heard her voice, I decided to protect myself for the first time. I hung up the phone. After all of this time, I finally had the power to not let my mother control me.

An Angel's Path

I traveled a path so alone,
You were not there,
I had no home.

I whispered to God, where are they now?
They must not love me,
Cried my silent child.

Please show me a sign,
Where could they be?
Am I not their miracle, please rescue me.

I shouted to God, "Please help me now!"
An Angel appeared,
"I'm here, my Child."

Touch me God, let me know you are here,
Take my hand and release my fear.

My parents have left me,
They've gone astray,
It's only me, therefore I pray.

He reached down and touched me,
"Blessed Be My Child,"
Travel this path I have chosen for you now.

A new path today,
With celebrating Angels.

My miracle child,
I have sent you light from every angle.

You travel a new path, but not alone,
Yes, they are gone,
But you have a new home.

My light surrounds you,
Let it shine so bright.

Now rest my child,
For the remainder of life.

Debra M. Luptak

CHAPTER NINETEEN

A Dance with Angels

Coming to face-to-face with my greatest fears, I have prevailed. There are treasures found in every journey and I will share mine with you. Along the way I have had to guard my child, as it was executed before I had a chance to put on my shield and fight as a warrior on a lifelong battlefield. My first craving was to find answers to my child's confusion. How was I to claim others as parents, when my instincts were taking me to another place? Deeply buried pain and fear were rising to my conscious level. A surface that I pretended was strong and was always in control. My emotions and regression became best friends. Tears were wiped away before others noticed pain. But my face wore pain even without the tears. There was no hiding my face. I could not hide the pain that crept in through my veins, through the pores of my skin. My face could not feel happiness. My smile was shallow. Joy was nonexistent. Happiness was foreign to me. It was a new feeling, a feeling I had never felt before; therefore it must be wrong.

Long-lived emotions were camping out in the deepest forests of my body and only when they wanted to surface was I challenged in coping with them, sorting them out, understanding them and letting them go. With no internal or external tools, I was unaware. What is this? What is happening to me? And when I figured out what these hidden emotional cysts were, I refused to get rid of them, as they had lived within in me for so many years that it was the only thing that was familiar to me. Even with the help of others expressing their support, compassion and guidance, this journey was still my own, something I had to fix, something I had to heal on my own.

I was so afraid to relive the past, to dig up the grave of my childhood, but no one could do that but me. First to understand it, then to acknowledge it, then to have a plan and follow through with the plan was the intention. Since my internal darkness had always been my master, bringing it to the surface to throw it away was a painful quest. Dealing with the inner me was my greatest fear. I had to dig into the center of my world, grab every piece of darkness in its entirety, throw it away and start over. Emotions poured out and filled the room. A flood of pain and fear extruded from my body. Exhausting all of my energies, I could sleep for days. But I had to return to myself the next day, the next week and month to only begin the process all over again.

Charged with determination, I became the extreme analyzer. I questioned everyone and everything in my path. I became the thinker. I was thinking overtime. Soon worry became my shield from the external world around me. I learned to wear the face and have the confidence of a strong woman. At first it was my safeguard against other evil people that came into my path, but over time I discovered that this was strength and it was coming from within me. It wasn't an act, it was truly who I was. I found myself the traumatized child who had grown into the self-defense expert.

With my intuition and external receptors I was able to channel a better awareness of hidden pain, understand it, feel it and then let it go. The results were beginning to feel like an award. Tapping into the infinity of emotions became a full-time job. Taking an hourglass and searching the pieces of my buried childhood piece-by-piece was, to say the least, overwhelming. The more I practiced the technique to get rid of the past, the more the emotions that were bottled up for years were slowly leaving my memories. I learned that I was allowed to keep my memories, but heal the emotions.

Healing is a different experience for all of us. At different phases of my healing I had visions of my childhood through external forces. For me, external stimulants brought rise to deeply buried emotions first and then the memories followed. It doesn't always take place in that order. All of us are different. Over time my body would bring to the surface the amount of pain, fear or other emotions that my body knew I could handle at any given time. A body's defense mechanism is to heal in moderation, not all at once. At least this is how it worked for me. I began taking intuitive leaps as I entered into adulthood. I was gifted with external stimulants that were positive, therefore giving me something to grab onto, and a new channel to filter through while healing.

Somehow I was finding my way back to a place of revelation and renewal: my center, which meant facing what had been hidden for years. It was time to uncover the past by bringing it to my conscious level so that I could make life changes and still care for others, namely my children. I had to embrace my present while finding what mattered from the past. It was like my past and present were miles apart and I had to realize that I was the one meeting them in the middle. I was revealing how I got here and at the same time seeking out a future, as a child, a mother and a wife.

I took many different paths, the paths that I thought were the right ones. Stubborn and full of determination, I believed I knew what was best for my child and my adult. Long stretches of time were spent in tears, releasing endless pains from the inner part of my soul. Allowing myself to breathe, to deeply inhale through the nose and exhale through my mouth over and over to calm my restless body. I revealed my deepest emotional and physical courage so that I could reshape my future. It was as if a hurricane was living deep within me and after years of facing the life threatening waters, I could finally find calmer seas.

And yet, because I have had my parents and siblings imprinted on my soul, the emotional connections were the veins that fed my soul, my spirit. I ran around this way, for what felt like thousands of years, and I still didn't know if I was somehow going to find my way back to survival. Survival meant that I had to take a step back and travel and explore new paths, to take risks, to try new things. It took emotional courage to want to heal, to realize that my interior needed redecorating. My exterior was nothing short of perfection, as it remains today. But the real work was facing the interior. To clean up the inside, which would not necessarily change my outward appearance, but embrace the things in life that mattered the most. Seeking self-affirmations is like painting a forest, leaving trails of leaves on your path so that when fear strikes you, you can turn and find your way back to your safe place. Perhaps like hunters who briefly encounter their prey and discover fear in their flesh. It is only then that they are forced to give up the chase and return to a protected place.

Never refuse to uncover the truth and its complexities. If you refuse to seek the truth, to find a stiller brook, the waters only get rougher and more rapid and then you submit yourself to even darker days ahead. Be your own warrior. Trust a mirror, trust a journal. Gently massage your soul every day. Let your body breathe deeply. Walk down park paths surrounded by nature. Let your ears hear, catching the sounds of the earth. Let your eyes see the full, vibrant foliage that surrounds a forest or a family who protects their offspring. Let your nose take in the fresh air. Capture a glimpse of a flock of birds flying across a clear sky. Force yourself to straddle your legs over a broken, weathered tree lying on the earth's soil. Fold your arms behind your head and lean up against the other tree still standing. Take in the earth's beauty around you.

Soon you will discover being alone is never alone. You are never alone. Remember, a candle loses nothing by lighting another candle. For a new beginning, you will embrace what fuels the soul and then you will discover what heals you. As each of us uses various channels to heal, I can only share the way I healed. The ultimate is to search for what matters, hang on to it, embrace it with every breath and don't let go. Because all of us are angels, some of us become aware and some remain angels unaware.

Only if you want to can you master your day. Only you can flee with the dreamers and find what stimulates you. Who are you and what roads do you want to travel? All of us go through journeys of hoping to find something better. There is something larger, a deeper being than ourselves. You can only do that by settling the past, packing it into a nice arrangement and putting it into the trunk of history. It's closure, my friend.

Leftovers of pain, fear and anger do not need to live within us as we shuffle through life. There is a better plan for all of us. We can acknowledge those emotions that may be holding us back. Grieve in our own space, within our own time parameters and heal. We can travel thousands of miles, whatever each of us

needs. We don't have to fall to the ground and sur-
render because the journey seems too difficult. Float
through your process, daydream, whatever works for
you. Don't deny your deeper spirituality. Without your
angels, the road you are traveling will be far more
difficult and tiring, beyond your imagination. Trust
and embrace your gifts, they are fuel for the soul.
Don't be an angel unaware. Follow your strengths and
hang on tight, they are your greatest assets. You are a
beautiful person and you need to feel that, acknowledge that you are good, and allow yourself to shine
from the inside out, brighter than the stars in a nighttime sky. Allow your spirit to take flight. Don't worry,
my child, a broken wing will heal.

Chapter Twenty

Forgiveness

Brought into my mother's world, she believed deep within her own soul that I was a Devil's child. Her illness, undetected, had pierced my existence. Singled out and being the first daughter born, destiny was dancing on a stage of evil for me. Every day every breath my little girl took was a breath of fear. The fear of death was staring back at me when I saw my mother's face. I was in my mother's emotional prison from the beginning of my life.

Never did I have a chance to stand up and fight against

the strongest being in my life, my mother. When I saw her face, the fear in my body forced me to stare back with no voice. I quivered and trembled as fear took over my body. When I saw her face the next time and every time thereafter, my body would slowly slide away from her, slumping into a fetal position, putting my arms around my head and knees to my chest and trembling until the beatings were over. Internally, I begged to the heavens for my torture to stop. Living every day with this woman, who should have cared and nurtured me, was horrifying.

My child had no voice. Silence was a way for me to survive. Darkness was all around me. Darkness had become my best friend. I learned that where there was darkness there was safety. Evil was playing with my life. Locking me up in a dark, small closet for the first three years of my life was her way to keep me hidden from the rest of the world. It was as if my mother saw me as this freak with three eyes. She believed she had "borned" a freak and she had to keep this freak hidden from the world, never to allow anyone to see me for I was cursed. I was the demon of her world and keeping me locked away in a closet was keeping her safe from her own evilness, her paranoid

schizophrenic behaviors. A delusion that has consumed her world.

Paranoid Schizophrenia:

*Paranoid Schizophrenics have systemized delusions and, fre-
quently, related auditory hallucinations (American Psychiatric
Association, 1987.) They usually show delusions of grandeur
and persecution, but may also show delusions of jealousy, in
which they believe that a spouse or lover has been unfaithful.
They may show agitation, confusion, and fear, and experience
vivid hallucinations that are consistent with their delusions.
The paranoid schizophrenic often constructs a complex or systemized delusion involving themes of wrongdoing or persecution.*

*A rarely used, related diagnostic category is paranoia (or "de-
lusional [paranoid] disorder," according to the DSM-III-R).
People may receive this diagnosis if they show a permanent,
"unshakable" delusional system that does not have the bizarre-
ness typical of schizophrenia. Persons with the disorder do not
show the confused, jumbled thinking suggestive of schizophrenia.*

Hallucinations, when present, are not prominent. Daily func-

*tioning in paranoia and in some cases of paranoid schizophre-
nia may be minimally impaired, or not impaired at all, so long
as the person does not act on the basis of his or her delusions.
The schizophrenia may go into remission. This may be the
point where there is no impairing at all, or not in touch with
the stressor that may have created the impairment of his or her
delusion in the beginning of the disorder.*

American Psychiatric Association, 1987

When Mother would drag me from the closet, grabbing my hair with the force of her large body and
arms, like a hunter would drag his prey, I was tortured because there was something wrong with me. I
was separated from other siblings and was not allowed
to be in their presence as she believed that I might
influence or possess them.

Now that I am a grown woman, I have learned to
close the gates of Hell. After forty-one years of living, sorting out the confusion, the pain and fear and
every other emotion imaginable, I am the miracle
child.

I have found it, harmony at last. After digging deep

into the depths of my soul, I have mastered the un-imaginable. My strength is now my reward. With only small amounts of pain now, it is manageable. I can continue this journey without fear, without worry. My tasks are now before me, clearer than before. Patience is no longer missing in the lost and found box of my mind. My search for clarity is now over. I can embrace the remainder of my life with new energies uncovered. With no apprehension, I can stand tall, as tall as the aged trees in every forest on earth. As the largest forests are full of maturity, so am I. I must celebrate. I must search for others to celebrate with me. Wisdom has been painted on every canvas I touch through my experiences. The signs that surround me have shown me this new path. Angels were always there, or I would not have survived, but now they gently take my hand and guide me somehow. Maybe that is what they were doing when I was a child, they were there all along.

Listen to your heart, as I have had to do. Unfold who you are; it has impressed me too. Some may not believe me, but your spirits are alive. Though they may be temporarily buried in a place you cannot find, you can find your spirit, just by being aware. Discover who you are. Take yourself on long walks, alone is not alone. Teach the world around you that you are a wonderful person. But more importantly, you must believe you are a good person. Let everyone know you have many gifts to share. When you have helped yourself, then it is much easier to lend a wiser hand to others.

My wish is to hold out my hand and touch each of you with the tools with which I have been taught. How did I do it? Facing my fears, acknowledging what I was feeling is real. Allowing myself to shed endless streams of tears. After my tears had flooded my surroundings, I could think more clearly. Closure needs to take place. Bringing closure to your past is the only means for a brighter future. Yes, we have many bumpy roads along the way, many roadblocks we must hurdle, but ultimately your strength will prevail.

I have done what no others thought I could do. Yes, my friend, it is a miracle. I have taken a catastrophic childhood and turned it into the most fortunate, most wonderful experience for myself. I have turned it into a miracle, Me. I have turned it into a gift that I can share with others in hopes of helping them muddle through their most difficult parts of life, in this case, childhood. I have proven to the world, and more importantly to myself, that I am a conqueror, not just a survivor. A survivor works his way through the trauma, barely coping with ongoing challenges, his struggle never ends. He gets caught up in the realm of the past. His line is snagged and the weight behind his line weighs far more than his ability to cut the line and start over. The paths he takes become long and exhausting; he finds himself at the end with nothing better.

A conqueror does much more than that. A conqueror learns not to allow the dark to creep in through the vulnerable entries of his spirit. Childhood trauma is much like a plague. It strikes unexpectedly. It becomes a contagious disease that is a sudden unwelcome. Evil causes trauma. It infests our bodies. It slaps you in the face as a child, asking that you have no reaction. That you just go through each day suffering in order to learn what physical and emotional pain really does to the veins and arteries in your body that ultimately lead to and from your heart. As you grow into adulthood, you are forced to relive your childhood. You are caught up in the experiences, the memories and the emotions. You spend much of your time searching for answers. As each segment unfolds, it stares at us as if evil wants to take us on in battle, in hopes that it will win.

The forces of good and evil have always been my struggle. Which road do I travel? Which has more power of persuasion over me? I felt many times that I was connected to evil and that good was not intended to be a part of my plan. But somehow I was able to tap into my courage and inner strength and go into battle with evil. I was drained. I was tired of feeling only dark emotions. Something from within was telling me that pain wasn't the only way to feel or to react. Something told me that my life did not have to be surrounded by anger, resentment, jealousy and fear at all times. I just always envisioned that this was my path and nothing good was going to travel my road. But that's the trickery of evil and trauma. Evil likes to trick you into believing it rules your life. It knows how to rise from an actual or so-called bad character or conduct around you, which in turn causes you the same discomfort and harm.

My reward for living a childhood hell is freedom and

teaching others to protect and save themselves in the fight for their lives. As I have unfolded my past, relived the experiences, identified with the forces of loss, I have put up a gripping fight.

My new mission is set before me. As angels gently take my hand, I am led down a new path, a path that will help others. A path where I can travel the world, tell my story to "Save the Children." Walk with me, allow me to take your hand and help your hearts heal. Let the quietness of earth surround you as I respect your fragile hearts. A woman of emotions, a woman of great wisdom, courage and strength, let me walk with you into the journey of healing. Let me help you dance with the angels. Let us celebrate letting go and discovering a deeper self.

I can teach others to find a lost love of themselves. I can show you your strengths, and where your courage lies unsettled within you. Let me help you bring alive your senses that are protecting you from harm. We can scream together, we can weep together, as I will be your strength until we uncover yours. I will not be passive, for I am unbelievably strong. I will show you how to search for an extension of yourself, something deeper than your conscious level. Let me teach you meditation. Let me show you that silence and being alone is not abandonment. As a tree falls in a forest, no one hears, but if you were there, you would hear.

Let me draw you the lesson of life, guiding you to shoot for your dreams. I would like to paint you, as I know what lies within you. We can bring good graces to the surface, to a conscious level so you can see without blinders. Let me toughen your instincts to unveil your senses, the senses of who you are. If I can teach you to see it and feel it, then I can teach you to do it.

Remember, a candle loses nothing by lighting another candle, it only creates more light. Let me be your candle of light.

A Mended Wing

Now it's time to travel,
Once again my child,
Your wings have mended,
Go fly the wild.

I have showed you signs along the way,
You have a new path,
Now don't astray.

Dive into life with your endless strength,
My gifts surround you,
No time to think.

Watch for signs,
As they surround,
My eagle child,
Never slow down.

Embrace your dreams,
For it's my gift to you,
And watch the predators escape this too.

I've reached down and touched you,
Healing your wing,
Now you may fly,
Like an eagle sings.

Leave your images frozen,
Far beneath the dirt,
I wish you no pain,
Only harmony on earth.

Your age is now timeless,
So use your wings to fly,
There are no more dark tunnels,
Your spirit is Alive.

Debra Luptak

MOTHER OF CHOICE

The little boy on the radio commercial for child abuse says, "I wish I had someone to call mommy and daddy." His dream, unlike the average child, is to have a mommy and daddy who love and care for him. He wants to stop wishing. The commercial is not only advertising child abuse and how it must be stopped, but also how adoption can save the children.

When my mother and father gave me up for adoption at the age of six, there was nothing in life so painful than to realize as a small child that my parents did not want me. I thought, if my mommy and daddy don't want me, who does want me? I believed even God didn't love me because he allowed my parents to torture me from the beginning of my life. Even with those thoughts, I still wanted to go back to my parents. I believed in my mind that they were going to come and get me someday and we would live hap-

191

pily ever after. I believed I would get to see my brothers and sisters again and that we would play together, laugh together and grow up together. My little girl wanted so much to remain with my parents, regardless of their daily torture that inflicted pain, bruises, tears, fears and sadness, because they were my parents.

Life doesn't always give us what we think we want most at any given time. I believe there was a higher purpose for me, and my parents raising the five of us children together was not part of the plan. I was forced at a very young age to cope with "new parents." People who were strangers, who I had never seen before, who were claiming to love me. How could a stranger love me?

Gael Entrikin, a professional social worker who helped children and adults every day as part of her career, became much more than that to me. Because I was already nine and considered an older child when I was adopted by a Minnesota family, I was extremely resistant to accepting strange people as my mommy and daddy. I did not want anyone to take the place of my parents, because they were coming to get me.

Gael Entrikin went beyond her professional responsibilities with me. She took me under her wing and helped me let go of my childhood, the stubborn concept that others could not take the place of my parents. She taught me that other people in the world, other than my parents, could love me. The ability to love a child, who is not biologically your own, is truly a gift of love.

I chose Gael as my "Mother of Choice." I found comfort in her words, her ability to take me into her arms and hold me as a child, a child who was lost, confused and sad. Her ability to provide direction for me, her ability to be stern with me when I was most rebellious, her ability to be compassionate when I needed to grieve, and her ability to step out of her professional role and be a mother figure to me, were gifts I received from Gael. God Bless this woman who took me under her wing and watched and supported me as I grew into a beautiful, strong, young woman. Thank You, Gael! You are my Mother of Choice!

GAEL ENTRIKIN, SOCIAL WORKER

*I*n *a country that claims to want what's best for children, it is unthinkable that there were 879,000 substantiated cases of abuse and neglect in the year 2000. Tragically some 1200 of the children involved died. All too often the survivors grew up with labels such as "sick," "sinful" and "criminal." Too many parents who have not had their own needs met are unable to meet their children's need for nurture and support, causing unseen damage to souls and psyches. Frequently their children become excessively passive, or aggressive in the search for a way to find love, a way to express their pain, or in finding a way to know who they are. It doesn't have to be this way.*

Recently a few of the "unknown statistics" have begun to speak out about the damage that was done to them, and the effect it has had on their lives. They are merely the tip of an iceberg in our midst, one many of us either deny or ignore.

Why do we not "see" the abuse of children, the impacts on their personalities, the damage to their adult lives? We need to know their stories, we need to learn from them, we cannot be a caring society until we can nurture all of our children.

When I first met Debra she was 11. Her pain was so great that she could not believe she was worth being loved. Her behavior was so rebellious that she needed to be hospitalized. Though she had been removed from her parents' negligence and abuse, she was not able to let anyone else get close enough to her to love her. It was important for her growth to realize where her issues came from and that her behavior was a way to cope. It is important for us to know how the behavior related to her self-image, and about her tenacious struggle to become who she is. Then we must become advocates for all children of abusive families, and adults still struggling with issues of childhood trauma.

Gael Entrikin, MSSW, LICSW (retired)

Author's Praises

I'm in shock. I've only known Debra a short time, but I never would have guessed that she's been through this kind of hell. She's a professional woman who carries herself with confidence, dignity and grace. Debra has been my friend and confidant, and her advice has been nothing but intelligent, balanced and full of love and compassion. And I value her opinion immensely. She has really come a long way in healing herself through her love for others. I'm truly astounded; she is an amazing heroine from whom we can all learn!

Kathy Glur

Deb and I have a saying, "If everyone plays right, it all works." For years I did not know how truly powerful that was, nor just how far she had come from where NOBODY played right, to where with a little honest, sincere, friendly, healthy trust and support to believe in herself (without being judged) she could overcome whatever it took - and has - to achieve her dreams. Yet as much as she thinks she has accomplished, she has but only begun her journey to the ultimate purpose for which she was put on this earth...and she will do it!

Keith Richard Kearney

197

In my 27 years of knowing Debra, I have never heard of such an emotional, compelling story of child abuse. From the straightaway we became dear friends, as I was inspired to help Debra as she worked through her heart-stopping experience. I was Debra's sounding board, her shoulder to cry on when she needed a friend. And now I look at Debra as a very strong, vital woman who has overcome tremendous obstacles in her life. Her book absolutely is a reality check of how a child can triumph into a courageous adult.

Renee Wiskow

We all have the choice to be devastated or motivated by the events in our lives. Debra has certainly chosen to be motivated to make life better for herself and other survivors of abuse. I am proud to know her!

Michelle Lason-King

Time, when relating to friends, has no bearing. We have only known Debra for a short time, but the depth of our friendship is profound. Debra is more than just a survivor. She has conquered her childhood past, and with the help of friends, has healed. Debra now offers her help so others may heal.

Steven & Patricia Carlson

Conclusion

My book is all to me. I have scribed the events of my soul. For many years the winds blew memories into my conscious awareness and the oceans consumed my tears. The wooded lands could hear my voice of fear as I traveled from history to become stronger than I had ever dreamed.

I was destined to find my place. For a number of years I traveled my journey without a destination. Although familiar to the humility and disappointment of watching childhood plans disappear into the winds, I suspected a real sense of connection with my own awareness of inner peace, my own individuality. The more I accepted the unexpected turns and twists of my wandering path, the more my self evolved.

Curious to rush to the end of my path to discover my inner connections to this world, patience unfolded around me. Wonder blossomed throughout the trees in the spring. Fall turned into stumbles and tangents and winter was my time and breathing space to rest.

The closer I was to the end of my path, the more I was drawn to learn more about myself and pursue a connection to my inner self. From the fountains of forgiveness, I set free years of resentment and anger against the wonder of my parents.

Now I have found closure. I have released the kite strings of time and they drift away from my present existence.

As nighttime descends and the shadows of evil are gone, I am now dancing in circles. I have sprouted into a new voice that can be heard. I can now stand at your door and blossom with the inner spirit gifted to me long ago by the works of my Lord.

All that I ask of you now is to please remember me.

Author's Comments

In order to maintain the respect and privacy of those involved, family, friends and professional names have been changed throughout my book. The names of my children—Brian, Shannon, Bryce and Shawn and my current husband, Stephen, as well as my name, Debra, have remained the same.

This book was written in my voice. The tenor and expressions reflect my adult perspectives and perceptions of my childhood and my adult life to my present age of forty-one. The events are real and connected to my memories and emotions.

If by chance you have found this book to be offensive, remember this story contains my childhood and adult experiences, my world. Even though parts of the book may be offensive to some, it is my intent that this book reach many areas of the world and many families and individuals who have suffered a similar childhood and let them know there is hope.

Although my childhood took place back in the 60's, sadly enough the same abuse is still happening today in many families. I hope my story will help bring public awareness to the seriousness of child abuse. If my book can inspire us to work together to save the children, then I have accomplished my intentions.

It is my dream to travel the world and be a voice for the children, the voice of the healing adult. I hope to reach out my hand to others who want and need to learn of my endurance. If I can share with you the gifts I have discovered along the way, which helped my own healing, then I have turned a horrific childhood into my greatest reward, helping others. Perhaps the ultimate plan for me was to initially suffer in childhood so that I could discover later in life how to reverse that gruesome experience and to become a strong adult, with the gift to teach and help others in their own paths of healing.

When I reunited with my biological father, he provided certain details of information regarding my earlier years of childhood. It was my father who assisted me in connecting some of the events of history with the memories and emotions I had carried as baggage for many, many years.

RESOURCES FOR HELP

National Child Abuse Hotline - The media plays a key role in getting the hotline number in the hands of children and adults who need help or answers to their questions about child abuse.
http://www.childhelpusa.org

Prevent Child Abuse America - State and Local Offices Latest Developments Contact Us, Doris Duke Charitable Foundation. This site funded by the Doris Duke Charitable Foundation, I Want to Help.
http://www.preventchildabuse.org

Child Abuse Prevention Services - Reporting Child Abuse - Help - How to Report Child Abuse Both the reporting party and the child who is allegedly being abused must reside in the same state for the following reporting...
http://www.kidsafe-caps.org/report.html

Child Abuse Prevention Association - CAPAs Mission. The mission of CAPA is to prevent and treat all forms of child abuse by creating changes in individuals, families and society which…
http://www.childabuseprevention.org

NNCC Child Abuse Database - Child Abuse. Click here for PDF help in viewing a PDF document. Bonding and Attachment in Maltreated Children: How Abuse and Neglect…
http://www.nncc.org

Sexual Abuse - PANdoras Box The Secrecy of Child Sexual Abuse Dr. Nancy Faulkner, advocates for the protection of children and prevention of child sexual abuse.
http://www.prevent-abuse-now.com.

VOICE - Victory Over Incest & Child Exploitation - As an organization, it is our mission to increase public awareness through education, support and protection for victims and preventions of victimizations. Our members are committed to providing education to the public of all ages to increase awareness of the crime and the injuries that incest and child exploitation causes to the victim.
http://www.avoice.info

ABOUT THE AUTHOR

Debra M. Luptak is a recognized professional in the computer information technology industry, with a background in psychology, sociology and graphic arts. Debra has recently been recognized as an "A+ Consultant" in her career. She owns and operates her own web design company, a business she originally started in Europe. As the mother of four sons, Debra made sure she gave her children something she never had, a wonderful childhood.

It is Debra's passion to travel the world and use her voice and her hands to reach out and help others unveil the memories of traumatized childhood in order to heal. She hopes to bring child abuse awareness to our society's surface, not only to save the children, but to help young children learn that there is help available.

Debra is currently writing her second book, which she hopes will be a helpful educational, step-by-step tool for those working through the healing process.